MICHAEL MOYNAGH & MICHAEL ADAM BECK

THE
21<u>st</u> CENTURY
CHRISTIAN

FOLLOWING
JESUS
WHERE
LIFE
HAPPENS

A FRESH EXPRESSIONS BOOK

The 21st Century Christian: Following Jesus Where Life Happens
Copyright © 2020 by Michael Beck and Michael Moynagh

Requests for information should be sent via
e-mail to info@freshexpressionsus.com. Visit
freshexpressionsus.org for contact information.

ISBN 978-1-7345081-1-6 (Paperback)
ISBN 978-1-7345081-3-0 (Kindle)
ISBN 978-1-7345081-2-3 (ePub)

Cover design: Ryan Tate
Interior design: Harrington Interactive Media
(harringtoninteractive.com)

Printed in the United States of America

The world around us has changed. The institutional church has lost much of its status and influence in the West, and we need to find new ways of reaching people with the Good News of Jesus Christ. Michael Moynagh and Michael Beck provide tested, practical guidance for leading people to Christ in the midst of a culture that is often suspicious of, and even hostile toward, the church. There is much we can learn here.

— **David F. Watson**, Academic Dean,
United Theological Seminary,
Dayton, Ohio

A short, punchy book packed with real-life examples of individuals and churches that have taken the plunge into following Jesus in innovative ways. Loads of friendly, accessible advice and memorable imagery for anyone who needs a nudge into reimagining how to join God's mission in their community. This is a generous and confident guide into the exciting unknown.

— **Lucy Moore**, Founder and Team
Leader of Messy Church at the Bible
Reading Fellowship

This small book gives a 21st century answer about how you can be a missionary disciple 24/7 as your live out your everyday life. The authors encourage you to practically consider how God can use who you are and what you do for his mission—not just on Sunday, but Monday through Saturday as well. It's full of practical insights and examples to achieve this for yourself and with others.

— **Dave Male**, Director of Evangelism
and Discipleship for the
Church of England

Imagine, fifty years in the future, a galaxy of small Christian communities enabled by the Spirit illuminates every corner of society. Beck and Moynagh provide a user-friendly manual for Jesus-followers who are eager to join the adventure of realizing this transformational vision. Readers will find in this book practical guidance based on proven experience in empowering 21st century disciples in diverse contexts. I pray this little book will reap a great harvest for the kingdom of God.

— **Dr. Susan Billington Harper**, National
Director of Church Advancement,
American Bible Society

Contents

Acknowledgements

Our gratitude to Barry Crane, Jon Davis, Will Donaldson, Simon Goddard, and John Valentine for their helpful comments on earlier drafts of the book, to Chris Backert for his encouragement, to Chris Morton for overseeing the publishing process, to Chad Harrington for the design and packaging. We are responsible for any shortcomings.

Rev'd Dr Michael Moynagh and Rev'd Dr Michael Beck, June, 2020.

WELCOME
This is for you!

You want to follow Jesus, but you don't know how. What to do? The quick answer is to become a "little Christ," which is where the word Christian comes from. "What a tall order!" you may think. "No wonder I don't feel up to it!"

If you doubt your ability to grow to be like Jesus, don't despair. Most other Christians feel the same—you are not alone.

We want to help you become a "little Christ" in a way you may not have considered before. It involves rethinking what it means to be mentored by Jesus and to learn from fellow Christians—and allowing this to happen in your everyday life.

Following Jesus has become like flying with one wing. We get lots of support and instruction within the church, but not much outside. This can send us plummeting toward the ground in a never-ending barrel roll, one in which we feel stuck going in spiritual circles. Unless we add a second wing—practical support where life happens—our Christian discipleship will never take off.

A gap has opened up between Christian teaching in the church and believers' everyday lives. What does it mean to go cycling as a Christian, for example? Who in your Sunday congregation sees your behavior among your cycling friends and can encourage you to stick to your Christian values? Who helps you to share your faith with fellow cyclists? It's scary to do these things on your own!

Does this gap strike a chord? If so, we are writing for you. We want to introduce you to a simple, practical, relational approach to being mentored by Jesus in the day-to-day rhythms of life—one that is both fresh and vintage.

It's vintage because it reflects what Jesus did. He taught his disciples in the midst of reality. For example, in Luke 18:15–17, Jesus showed his disciples how to treat children and connected this to the kingdom of God. Where did his teaching happen? Not inside a synagogue—the church of his day—but in a public setting. Neither did it happen mainly in private, one-on-one conversation, but rather largely in community with others.

Jesus went beyond private conversations to teach his disciples in day-to-day life as they were going about the normal business of living together. Here, we've remixed his practice to suggest a fresh, 21st century approach to discipleship.

Our starting point is that the real heroes of the church are everyday Christians who live their faith where life happens. If you've picked up this book, you're our hero!

With this book, we hope to support you on your journey of following Jesus with:

- A *compass* to point you in the right direction.
- A *map* to help you plot a route that works for you.
- Some *food* to sustain you along the way.
- The *address* of your destination so that you know what to look out for.

Most of all, we want to show you how you can follow Jesus, within your everyday comings and goings, *with one or more friends*. It is hard work, even soul-destroying, to follow Christ on your own. That's why so many Christians get disheartened. But if you do it with a friend, everything changes!

It is hard work, even soul-destroying, to follow Christ on your own.

In the pages of this book, we'll show you how the Great Commandment to love others can come alive in ways you never expected. You'll discover how the Great Commission—to share the Christian faith with others—can be so natural and simple that anyone can do it. You'll see how faith, mission, and church—big Christian themes—come together in daily situations.

Jesus came that we might have fullness of life (John 10:10). Might this be your moment? An opportunity to explore how your life could be richer than you ever imagined?

Both of us work with Christians who are reinventing discipleship for the 21st century. We'll share with you what we've learned from them. What we are writing about is not theory—it is what people are doing in practice on the ground, and it's working.

Rev'd. Dr. Michael Moynagh is a minister in the Church of England and is based at Wycliffe Hall, Oxford. In the early 1990s, he led a church that was one of the first in the UK to start an intentional teenagers' congregation. He has been involved in new types of Christian community for over twenty years, learning from the "pioneers" involved, and writing extensively about them. He is sometimes known as "the theologian of fresh expressions of church," and has an international consulting and teaching ministry.

Rev'd. Dr. Michael Beck is also a minister and author. He came to faith as a street-kid, redeemed by Jesus from a life of incarceration and addiction. He serves a traditional United Methodist congregation in Wildwood, FL. The heroes of Michael's story are the everyday Christians of his church who have joined him in cultivating over a dozen new Christian communities throughout the area in the normal places where they do life. Michael now serves on the Fresh Expressions US team and is Director of the Fresh Expressions House of Studies at United Seminary. He helps church leaders across the US follow Jesus in new and exciting ways.

CHAPTER 1

21st Century Discipleship

"There has to be more to being a Christian than showing up for worship, participating in Bible studies, or serving on a church committee. Is this the highpoint of following Jesus?"

Many have been asking a similar question lately. They articulate that something seems lacking in their experience of church. There is an odd sense that God has invited us to a wild adventure, an exciting journey of great challenges and wonderful vistas of possibility, but we are stuck at the base camp.

As Christians, we long to make an impact on our communities. We want to offer contributions that make the world a better place.

But how can we do this?

Across the globe, church leaders say that one of the greatest challenges for the church is *discipleship*. As we described in the introduction, discipleship is about learning and living out the way of Jesus in the world. We are all Christians in the making, on a journey toward spiritual maturity in Christ.

We are all Christians in the making, on a journey toward spiritual maturity in Christ.

Many churches today encourage discipleship mainly by imparting biblical knowledge in a church setting. Yet while this is important, discipleship also takes place through socialization. We learn from other Christians as we do life together and respond to real life pressures.

We don't just learn to memorize biblical passages; rather, we learn how to walk, how to talk, and how to love. This process is not limited to a church facility or a classroom, it can happen literally anywhere.

Discipleship also is a missional phenomenon. As we mature in Christ, we discover a deep sense of joy in loving others and sharing our faith with them. Jesus prepared his disciples for this activity on a global scale (Matt. 28:18–20). As we said in the introduction, he taught them in the midst of everyday life.

In fact, much of what we have called discipleship is in some ways foreign to how Jesus nurtured his disciples in the faith. We want to re-appropriate the essential practices of Jesus and contextualize them for our current reality.

Here is a 21st century way to follow Christ. We will explore these points in depth as we go:

- Find a friend (or more than one) in a corner of your life.
- Prayerfully discover a simple way to love the people around you.
- Deepen relationships with them.
- Share your feelings about Jesus when opportunities arise.
- Encourage those coming to faith to form a small Christian community where they are, and connect them to the wider church.

Anyone can do this!

Let us share some stories (though the names are disguised) to illustrate what we mean.

Tim met with a small group of young adults who'd dropped out of church. One of them loved canoeing. So his group advertised free canoeing on social media, and then paid for the canoes.

Families who didn't go to church gathered to canoe on Saturday afternoons, and then hung out together over a picnic or barbecue. One of the young adults would tell the children a Bible story, while parents listened in.

After a while Tim said, "I see you enjoy these stories. If you want more, I will be at home on Tuesday evenings for 'food and story'." A small group gathered. They explored stories about Jesus, learned to pray, and are becoming a Christian community in Tim's home.

For Tim, canoeing was not just a means to evangelism, it was worthwhile in itself. It led to friendships, which had intrinsic value. Exploring Christ was icing on the cake. If no one had come on Tuesday evenings, the cake would still have been worth eating.

Meghan and Heather were older women who taught teenagers to cook. Meghan knew the teenagers, Heather enjoyed cooking—a perfect combination. The teenagers would eat together with them afterwards.

The first time this group came together, the women asked permission to thank God for the food. After a while, the teenagers were invited to write their own "thank you" prayers, drop the pieces of paper into a cooking bowl, pass around the bowl, select a folded piece of paper, and read out the prayer. In time this was expanded to "request" prayers.

As "spiritual" conversations developed over the meals, the teenagers began discussing stories about Jesus. Slowly the group travelled toward Christ and became a small worshipping community.

Or consider the example of Mack, a young adult who went cycling with friends. Some of the cyclists' partners, who didn't enjoy cycling, organized for everyone to eat together when they got back. The cyclists were enjoying their passion while building relationships together. Those who organized and prepared the meals were also operating in their passions. Over time, they formed community around their common interests.

If you were doing something like this, you could theme the meal-time conversations and call them, "Chat with a difference." Members of the group might text a topic in advance, discuss it, and then ask, "If God exists, what would *he* think?" "Or if a spiritual guide was listening, what might *she* think?"

Take the idea a step further. Why not host conversations on Zoom? Use social media to gather people with a common interest in politics, or in reading Shakespeare's plays, or in a music genre, and Zoom about it for an hour.

If the spiritual temperature rises and some people want to take a next step, you could start a Zoom conversation at a different time for them to explore Christ a bit more. Chapter 5 will show how easy this can be! Anyone can do it!

Ideas to whet your appetite

Wildwood United Methodist Church in Florida has started over fourteen new Christian communities in the past eight years, including:

- *Arts for Love.* Art enthusiasts gather to pray, worship, and create art together.
- *Blessing Bags.* A group worships and prays as members collect and distribute necessary items for people experiencing homelessness.
- *Burritos and Bibles.* Seekers gather in Moe's Southwest Grill for burritos, prayer, Scripture, and Holy Communion.
- *Church 3.1.* Young professionals run 5k (3.1 miles), pray, and have a conversation about some verses from Scripture.
- *Connect.* A church for children involves fun activities, breakfast, Jesus stories, and worship in the local Community Center.
- *Faithfully Fit.* Health enthusiasts meet in the park for prayer, devotions, and walking the track.
- *Higher Power Hour.* Seekers in recovery explore spiritual practices including prayer and poetry.

- *Mascara Mondays.* A handful of women gather in the local coffee shop for prayer and Bible reflection.
- *Paws of Praise.* Dog lovers gather in the local dog park for prayer, worship, Scripture, and play.
- *Shear Love at Soul Salon.* A pop-up salon offers free haircuts, prayer, and a Bible reflection.
- *Skate. Pray. Repeat.* A group of friends gather at indoor rinks and outdoor tracks to skate, pray, and share their faith.
- *Tattoo Parlor Church.* Seekers receive faith-based tattoos and worship Christ with Holy Communion.
- *Trap Stars for Jesus.* Ex and current drug dealers learn how to start legitimate businesses, with prayer and Scripture mixed in.[1]

When COVID-19 struck, they cultivated new digital communities:

- *Yoga Church Digital.* Rather than meeting in a studio, a live devotional and yoga

....

1. Michael Beck, *Deep Roots, Wild Branches: Revitalizing the Church in the Blended Ecology* (Franklin, TN: Seedbed Publishing, 2019).

practice was broadcasted into people's homes through Facebook and YouTube.

- *Supper Table Church.* Young parents who found themselves isolated in quarantine suddenly became homeschool teachers overnight. So these parents prepared themed meals, placed a screen at the supper table, and joined together digitally to eat, converse, pray, and share ideas.
- *Paws of Praise Digital.* Animal lovers gathered with their pets on screens using Zoom rooms to share in conversations and showcase their pets' unique personalities.
- *Living Room Church.* A network of Christians met digitally from their homes to pray, worship, have communion, and share in sermonic conversations.

Might this be what "church" looks like for some new Christian communities? Animal lovers walk their dogs in twos and threes at various times of the week, for example, and then all come together online—the goal is analog and digital church combined!

People from outside the church join these Wildwood communities. Anyone interested is introduced to Jesus as part of a richer life. A number of people are journeying to faith.

We hope and pray some of them will connect with the wider church and start further communities themselves.

In 2016, Christ Church in Bayston Hill on the edge of Shrewsbury, England, was serving people outside church in the following ways:

- *Coffee in the Living Room.* A weekly cafe for patients of the local medical practice.
- *Messy Church.* A monthly all-age church combining craft, Bible story, prayer, and food.
- *Outlook.* A gathering for the over-55s, with a monthly guest speaker and refreshments.
- *Senior Citizens Lunch.* A meal followed by a few hymns, prayers, and a short talk.
- *Stepping Out.* A group formed around walking.
- *Tiddlywinks.* A mini Messy Church for families with children under five years old.
- *Zone.* A weekly gathering for teenagers.

In 2010, this church was reaching up to 250 people. By 2014, the church was regularly in touch with over 500 people.

From Florida and England to the Protestant Church of the Netherlands (PKN), these new communities include:

- Home-based missional communities in Rotterdam to share lives and begin discipleship.
- Space for migrants in Nieuwegein to meet and worship in an intercultural environment.
- A neighborhood living room in Zwijndrecht to build community through activities for all ages.
- A community in Ede for social entrepreneurship and local initiatives.
- Meals, Messy Church, and arts to draw generations together in Den Haag.
- A new monastic community in Jorwerd creating spaces for quietness and meditation in a rural area.
- A community in Amsterdam for spiritual seekers with meals, events, and conversations.
- Music, theatre, and storytelling involving spiritual seekers in the rural area of Schagerbrug.

Similar kinds of new Christian communities are springing up across the globe, right where life happens. But they are forming alongside and in relationship with existing congregations.

Think of the original church as a hub with small satellite communities around it. Each is led by Christians following Jesus in a 21st century way. Over time they began to link together face-to-face, online, or both. Through these communities, God's love seeps into the nooks and crannies of the surrounding neighborhood.

These new communities are not better than the existing congregations to which they are connected. They are just different, with different ministries and missions. Older congregations safeguard and pass on the tradition. New Christian communities express the tradition freshly in other contexts. Both flourish alongside each other in mutual love and support.

In technical language, new Christian communities are creating social capital— networks of relationships among people, which allow society to function more effectively.

These relationships are valuable in themselves; they are not merely an excuse for sharing the gospel. But they are also gateways to more. They open doors to a fuller life, if people want it.

They are like a field with a beautiful view. You can stay in the field if you wish, or you can walk through it to another field, with an even more breathtaking horizon.

Jesus came that people might have breathtaking views—life in abundance (John 10:10). Through 21st century discipleship, this offer is extended to people outside the church.

Reasons why this can work for you

Following Christ in this way transforms discipleship. First, it helps you to love people as Jesus taught (Mark 12:28–31). Love is more than warm feelings or a happy conversation. It's practical. And practical love has to be organized.

Imagine a family and all the love within it—getting the children to school, marshalling the evening meal, arranging a family treat, preparing a birthday party, or celebrating a holiday. This love doesn't just happen. It has to be organized.

Practical love has to be organized.

Now of course you can arrange it on your own. Many single parents do so brilliantly. But how many would prefer to have a partner? It's easier and more fun to love people when you do it with someone.

A young man had returned to Christ and was enthusiastic about his more purposeful life. He decided to give away free donuts each week to people on a small building site near his work. He did this for a while, but then stopped.

What he needed was a friend who was on the same page to join him. They could have encouraged one another, debriefed together, had a laugh, and stood in for each other if one was away. Love is best organized with friends.

Secondly, 21st century discipleship gives focus to your Christian life. For many churchgoers, following Jesus is like playing basketball without a hoop, or soccer without goal posts.

You pass the ball, but to no purpose. After a while you get bored, wander off the court or field, and melt into the crowd walking by.

Often Christians merge into everyday life and become discipled *by the world.* To lead a distinctive Christian life, it helps to have Christian projects, supported by Christian friends, in the contexts where we live. These projects give discipleship a Spirit-shaped focus, through which the kindness of Christ can touch people nearby.

Thirdly, this focus helps you to grow in Christian maturity. There is no better way to cultivate Godly character than to be on mission, in life, with fellow Christians.

Being "on mission" means turning away from yourself and toward others. Faith is stretched and prayer intensified as you organize love without being sure the initiative will work. You learn patience and other fruits of the Spirit when you overcome obstacles and face setbacks.

"In life" means sharing in the heartaches as well as the joys of the people you love. Looking for God in both the thunderstorms and the rainbows draws you away from naive answers.

If Christ is Lord of everything, however bleak, you are impelled to ask, "So what does Christ's reign look like in this disappointment and in that sadness?" You learn to cope with the ambiguities of biblical faith and how they play out in real life.

"With fellow Christians" means you have companions to challenge and encourage you, discern God's will with you, and hold you to account in your walk with Jesus.

Most people who see you in church on Sunday have no idea how you behave the rest of the week. But Christians who join you on mission in everyday life can see all too vividly what you're like, which is a huge spur to live with integrity.

Christians who participate in short-term mission placements often describe the transformational benefits to their faith. They are exposed to new world views and diverse perspectives. Their false assumptions are challenged. They describe a renewed sense of meaning and deeper purpose for their lives. 21st century discipleship can have similar effects—but the "placement" is longer term.

Fourthly, think of all the riches of the church—how it has blessed you and many others. It is:

- Your spiritual birthplace and home.
- A community of friendship, care, and support.
- A source of spiritual growth through sung worship, preaching, the sacraments, prayer retreats, small study groups, conferences, and large celebrations and festivals.
- A servant to the neighborhood and beyond through outreach activities, a ministry of presence alongside those in need, a participant in movements of

social and environmental justice, and a
gift of time and money.
- The custodian of a rich heritage of faith.
- The inspiration for beautiful art, music,
literature, and architecture.

But listen to your friends. How often have
you heard it said, "Jesus is okay. The church is
the problem"? The church has enriched life
in the past and continues to do so today. Yet,
swarms of people now see it as a stumbling
block.

That can change when you bring the
church to people where they are, in a manner
they respect. Their experience of the church
will be you and your friends loving them and
exploring with them a fuller life. Your love will
repaint their negative ideas about the church.

Church won't be that strange institution
over there. It will be up close. It will be people
they know—people:

- who organize practical love.
- who invite them to explore spirituality in
ways that make sense to them.
- who welcome them into God's home and,
importantly, allow them to furnish this
spiritual home in *their* style.

Church will stop being out of reach. It will become accessible and relevant. People will be loved into faith by starting not in our church, but in their world.

> **PEOPLE WILL BE LOVED INTO FAITH BY STARTING NOT IN OUR CHURCH, BUT IN THEIR WORLD.**

Finally, it is easy to start.

A group of young adults gave away free cakes to flavor their neighborhood with kingdom generosity. They asked people to suggest who might receive a cake—someone's birthday, a wedding anniversary, passing a driving test, or recovering from an illness. They called themselves "Random Acts of Cakeness."

Anyone can do this! Might you try something similar? You never know where that first step could lead.

The benefits for others are obvious, but they are also obvious for you as a Christian in the making. Love, focus, growth, relevance, and simplicity are five reasons to walk with Jesus in a 21st century way:

- Your LOVE will be organized and therefore more fruitful.
- Your discipleship will have a sharper FOCUS.
- You will GROW in your faith.
- The church will be more RELEVANT to your friends.
- Starting can be as SIMPLE as giving away cakes.

This is how following Jesus can center and drive every area of your life.

Making it work for you

21st century discipleship is for anyone, no matter what they are "into." In the network society, people form relationships around a vast diversity of hobbies, passions, and interests.

- Focused on work? New Christian communities have become windows to heaven with office workers, patients of a medical practice, and (where it's allowed) in schools.
- Concerned about people experiencing homelessness? Women who have been abused? Asylum seekers? Teenagers on drugs? People with learning difficulties?

Or simply your friends? A small team can pay attention to them, love them, build community with them, introduce those interested to Jesus, encourage a safe and supportive Christian community to emerge, and bring this community as a gift to the wider church.

- Passionate about the environment or social justice? You can listen to people outside the church who echo your heart, find ways to work together, form community as you do so, and explore how Christian spirituality can add color to your shared concern.
- Into sports? Dog walking? Singing? Repairing bikes? Christians in community are bringing people alive around these and other interests.
- Live in a village or small town? In a neighborhood with deep poverty? Or belong to an ethnic minority? New Christian gatherings are giving these settings their voice too.

New Christian communities reveal Christ *any*where—with *any*one. They provide an inkling of heaven—a rich variety of people, clothed in a wealth of different cultures, united in a single family, gathered around creation's nerve center of love.

Ephesians 1:23 promises that when Christ returns, he will fill—or complete—all things. When Christians, as the body of Christ, start new Christian communities in the myriad domains of life, they signpost this future. They demonstrate that there is no sphere where Christ and his church cannot make their home.

In Pittsburgh, Pennsylvania, a young adult described how he had been raised in a Christian family but drifted away from the church in his late teens.

He loved computer games. In one game he had to gain weight to cross a bridge, and a message told him that he could cross the bridge for free if he watched a video. The video was all about grace.

The young man watched it and was then invited to an online Bible study group, which he attended. Later, he decided to reconnect with the church off-line. "And here I am now," he said, "discussing intentional Christian community."

Christ can be present in communal form in *every* section of life, even a computer game! So:

- Find one or more friends and become a micro-congregation where life happens.
- Prayerfully discover a simple way to love the people around you and make your faith practical.
- Strengthen your friendships with them.
- Share your thoughts and feelings about Jesus as part of a fuller life.
- Encourage those coming to faith to form a Christian community where they are and become gifts to the wider church.

When you do this, you will bring together your faith, God's loving mission to the world, and the church. Don't put faith, mission, and church into different compartments. Join them up and follow Jesus in a 21st century way.

The next chapters describe four items that will help you navigate this path of discipleship—a compass, a map, food for the journey, and the address of the destination. Chapter 6 will show you how to be realistic, Chapter 7 will get you started, and Chapter 8 is an epilogue for church planters.

Get ready! Your Christian experience may never be quite the same.

CHAPTER 2
A Compass

Sometimes following Christ can feel like having two personalities. One is based on church—Sunday worship, joining a committee, and perhaps a small group or Bible study during the week. The second is about life—work, friends, home, and interests.

For most, the two barely overlap. How often have you thought, "I wish Sunday and Monday were more strongly connected"? Well, 21st century discipleship makes that connection. Church and life intertwine, as we believe God intends them to do.

As you do church in a part of your daily life, remember again these simple movements on the journey:

- you find a friend (or more)
- prayerfully discover a simple way to love the people around you
- deepen relationships with them
- share your feelings about Christ as part of a fuller life, and
- encourage those finding faith to form a small Christian community where they are and connect to the wider church.

All you need are four items for the journey—and lots of prayer. The first item is a compass. A compass is essential because it will help you start in the right direction. Without a compass you risk getting lost, but with a compass you can navigate the journey.

The points of the compass are four values, which will give you reasons for what you are doing and steer you in the right direction. Those values are *being missional, being contextual, being formational,* and *being ecclesial.*

Two women wanted to open a café to connect with people outside the church, but didn't know how. They wanted to be *missional.* One day they heard that the local medical practice wanted their church to help run a drop-in center for lonely and anxious patients.

Here was the answer to the women's prayers! They started a Thursday morning cafe for the doctors' patients. Each week, fifty or more people chatted together, played board games, enjoyed each other's company, and felt noticed and accepted. They were responding to the needs emerging from the community. They were being *contextual.*

The church's healing team got to know those involved in the cafe and offered prayer for those who needed it. They were growing spiritually together. They were being *formational* because they were being formed in Christlikeness.

Rather than getting invited to Sunday church, the patients tasted church during the week. By forming Christian community right where they were, they were being *ecclesial* (the Greek root word means "a called-out assembly or congregation").

The two women were following Christ in a contemporary way. Twenty or more years ago, doing church in the form of a "medical cafe" would hardly have crossed their minds. Now, more and more Christians are teaming up with others, bringing a slice of church to the people near them, and enriching their lives.

You can do the same.

- Your Christian life will be more fun because you'll share it with a friend.
- Your discipleship will have a focus.
- Your life in the church and in the world will come together.

Be missional

The first value point of the compass is what we call being *missional*. This is about engaging with people outside the Christian family. The idea is simple: with one or more friends, spread love to people who don't normally go to church.

Doing this reflects the passion of God. Christopher Wright, an Old Testament scholar, says that mission is one of the big themes holding Scripture together. Think about it . . .

The Bible presents:

- God with a mission (Ps. 86:9).
- humanity with a mission (Gen. 2:15).
- Israel with a mission (Gen. 12:1-3).
- Jesus with a mission, and (Lk. 19:10).
- the church as an extension of Jesus' mission (Jn. 20:21).

The aim of all this mission is that the entire creation should flourish through God's infectious generosity.[2] When you go out to others in organized love, you flow with what God is doing in the world and what he wants for it.

> **WHEN YOU GO OUT TO OTHERS IN ORGANIZED LOVE, YOU FLOW WITH WHAT GOD IS DOING IN THE WORLD AND WHAT HE WANTS FOR IT.**

Have you noticed that Jesus was crucified outside the city gate, where the remains of the temple sin offerings were burnt (Heb. 13:11–12)?

. . . .

2. Christopher J. H. Wright, *The Mission of God: Unlocking the Bible's Grand Narrative* (Nottingham: IVP, 2006), 64-68.

In the Old Testament, the temple, at the heart of the Holy City, was seen as the central location of salvation. There the priests offered sacrifices on behalf of the people to make amends for their sins. The sacrificial remains were burnt outside the city, well away from this focus of Israelite faith.

So when Jesus died outside the city gate, he died on the religious periphery, not at the religious center. Flanked by the two thieves and surrounded by Roman soldiers, he died in solidarity with people who were beyond the edge of the religious institution.[3]

The book of Hebrews urges, "Let us, then, go to him outside the camp . . ." (Heb. 13:13). The recipients of this letter were invited to join Jesus in the place where he had died—outside the city gate.

They were to find Jesus not at the center of institutional faith, but at the edge, among people outside the religious system. And we can do the same. When we do mission today, we encounter Christ among the people who are outside the church.

If you sometimes feel that God is a bit distant, that your Christian experience is

---

3. Orlando Costas, *Christ Outside the Gate: Mission beyond Christendom* (Eugene, OR: Wifp & Stock, 2005), 189.

rather prosaic, and that your spiritual energy has sagged, might it be that you are focused too heavily on the church, on the religious center?

If you want a spiritual pick-me-up, discover what Jesus is doing outside the church and join it. Seize the opportunities he is creating to bring hope, love, and abundance of life to people who have not yet come to know him. Be missional.

And be comfortable with being outnumbered. Involve more people who don't go to church than those who do.

Involve more people who don't go to church than those who do.

That's how Anna began when she led an explorers' course for people interested in the Christian story. She gathered people with a spiritual openness around a shared meal, presented stories from the life of Jesus in a simple way with a couple of songs mixed in, and invited participants to have conversations around those stories. When the course finished, participants said, "We love these evenings, the discussion, the food, and the Christian music. If the church was like this, we'd come."

Anna replied, "Church can be like this. Let's keep meeting on Thursday evenings, with food, discussion, and Christian songs, and discover what it means to follow Christ." So the evenings continued.

Then some churchgoers joined in. Unintentionally, the new arrivals changed the atmosphere. They assumed Christian knowledge the others didn't have. They asked questions that had never crossed the seekers' minds. And they used religious language that baffled the group. Gradually the initial members drifted away.

Don't think you need lots of Christian helpers. Too many Christians may wreck what God is doing! Start with just a few friends. Organize practical love. And don't worry that most people involved don't go to church. You'll discover Christ among them.

Be contextual

This part of the compass means fitting your context, doing what people around you feel is appropriate. Pay careful attention to the context. What are the language, symbols, and stories of these people? What are the customs and rituals they practice? Where do people gather for community? Rather than importing language and ideas from your own context or trying to recreate church in a way familiar to you, let it emerge organically with the people involved. Do this by simply using:

- your practical love
- your relationship building
- how you share the gospel (if people are interested), and
- the form the new Christian community takes (if it emerges).

Adam gathers monthly with a group of classic car enthusiasts. They meet in a garage with a cafe attached. During the summer they bring their cars and exchange stories. In the winter, they watch films about classic cars.

As people leave, Adam offers those who want it a short, written "thought for the day" on a theme related to classic cars, such as restoration (because they are restoring their cars).

One month, he invited them to bring a car part they thought was "fearfully and wonderfully made" (Ps. 139:14). They exchanged notes. They are now having discussions on the theme of "rust"—what is rusty in life as well as in their cars? In time, Adam hopes to work with some of them on "classic car spirituality."

All this is entirely appropriate for those involved. But with a different demographic, he would have needed a different approach.

Adapting how we form community around people outside the church is not how we normally arrange a congregation. More often, we tailor the church to suit the people inside the church. When, where, and how the congregation meets—music, length of sermon, and so on—are all designed with us worshippers in mind.

Having got it just as we like, we then invite others—"Come and join us." But this is an invitation to come on *our* terms. Can we be surprised if they politely decline? "It works for you," they think, "but not for me."

We are asking nonbelievers to jump the cultural hurdle. Yet, as Alan Hirsch and Dave Ferguson remark, we are sent to them—they are not sent to us.[4]

We start with people outside the church and what connects with them.

Being contextual is the opposite of "come and join us." We don't start with the church and how we like it. We start with people outside the church and what connects with them.

4. Alan Hirsch and Dave Ferguson, *On the Verge: A Journey into the Apostolic Future of the Church* (Grand Rapids, MI: Zondervan, 2011), 73.

We do what Jesus did. He immersed himself in Jewish life and showed people what it was like to follow God in their culture (Jn. 1:14).

Jesus was born a Jew, he died as a Jew, he was resurrected as a Jew, he ascended into heaven as a Jew, and he is next to his Father now still as a Jew.

Just as Jesus did not leave his Jewishness behind when he entered his Father's presence, his followers do not leave their cultures behind when they come to the Father. They bring their passions and lifestyles to him, and let the Spirit transform them.

A teenager offered his skateboarding to God as a form of prayer and worship. He commented, "I never knew God could be interested in my skateboarding"—there was no gap between life and God for him! What if we could understand that skateboarding can be a spiritual practice, one around which a new Christian community could form? By tending to the context, understanding people's passions, hobbies, and interests in the normal rhythms of their lives, we can close that gap.

Be formational

Jesus expects his followers to form disciples. Being formational is the third point of the compass. Through the Spirit, followers are to help other people come to faith and grow in Christ-likeness (Matt. 28:16–20). You can't force this, of course. But you can pray that this Great Commission will bear fruit among the people you love.

Start with your "hidden curriculum." This is your taken-for-granted way of doing things, such as how you lovingly serve people. Perhaps it is the special attention you pay to someone frequently overlooked. Perhaps it is the causes you are drawn to give yourself to.

This Christ-like attitude will rub off on others. Influenced by you, they will keep an eye out for those overlooked people and causes too. They will start following Jesus implicitly before committing to him explicitly.

Being formational is simply about taking next steps in your spiritual journey together. Often this emerges from the group itself. People begin to share about struggles they are having or begin asking questions about spirituality. Also, you can provide opt-in experiences along the way.

Let's say you have started gathering with a group of people around some common interest or shared practice. Community is really beginning to form as you meet together.

As a next step, why not introduce themed conversations?

A group of men wiped away graffiti, cleared up rubbish, and tidied grassed-over areas to improve the local environment. They then adjourned to the pub for a drink.

One of them had the idea of theming their conversations around "continuous improvement," the mantra of the nearby Toyota factory. How could they "continuously improve":

- In their environmental concern?
- As fathers?
- As partners?
- At work?
- In their friendships?

Why not offer "conversations with a difference"? Suggest that people take turns to choose a topic—an item in the news, their football team, a film, a favorite TV program, or a celebrity they follow. After discussing it for a while, ask: "If God exists (or a spiritual leader dropped in), what would they think about our discussion?"

One woman working with young people remarked, "This is so easy! I'll get two tables. On one I will write 'Love Island', a popular

British TV program. On the other I will write the name of a celebrity. I will invite the young people to select a table, discuss what's been happening, and include that question in their conversation."

Themed conversations can be a first step to sharing Jesus. But of course growing disciples doesn't stop there. New believers will need encouragement and support to mature in the faith. In particular, they will need help in discovering the radical, transforming power of the gospel in their day-to-day lives.

In contextually appropriate ways, being formational is about going further in the journey of becoming *Christians in the making*. We are being formed in the way of Jesus as we journey through life together. Over time, you can introduce central spiritual disciplines like prayer, meditation, reading Scripture, Holy Communion, and so on.

Does this all sound rather difficult? Don't worry! Chapter 4 will show how easy it can be. Even non-churchgoers can do it!

Be ecclesial

This is "churchy" language for starting a new Christian community among people coming to faith, and connecting them to the wider church.

Instead of inviting enquirers to church on Sunday, you can encourage them to form an expression of church where they are—face to face, by video, or using a hybrid of the two. They could be a new congregation, community, or group within a local church, or a new church with links to other churches.

This may not be as difficult as you think. Perhaps you are involved in an outreach activity, such as a parenting support group. Why not add a voluntary "spiritual growth" session after the meeting?

You could light a candle, play some gentle music, provide some cards with prayers or spiritual sayings, and invite people to meditate on the cards for a few minutes. Parents would be free to leave after the regular program or stay behind if they wished.

You have already done the hard work of gathering people. Now add a flavor of church for those who want it. As spiritual interest grows, you could ask the group how to build on what you've begun.

Take the church to people where they are! You'll be amazed: it's much easier than bringing the people to church.

And now that we have learned how easy meet-ups by video can be, the opportunities are endless!

As people walk a journey to faith in their own Christian community, they can enrich the original church by joining it periodically for worship, sharing their ideas, time and talents, and contributing financially. A new worshipping community may even be the means of revitalizing an older congregation.

When new Christian communities ripple out to different networks at times, in places, with agendas, and in styles that resonate with those they are trying to reach, the church—with its offer of a fuller life—becomes more welcoming and inclusive.

Like Wildwood and Christ Church in the last chapter, let your church be a hub at the center of a wheel. Encourage your members to start new Christian communities. Link them together to make a rim. And put in spokes that connect the rim to the original congregation.

These links and spokes could include:

- joint social events like a family fun day or harvest supper
- combined evening courses on biblical and other themes
- shared prayer retreats

- all-together worship at Easter and on other occasions, and
- joint mission initiatives, such as campaigning for a better environment.

Be ecclesial. Start new Christian communities where people are, with an agenda and style that works for them, and let these communities be gifts to the church-at-large.

Tear down the walls!

Think about this. All churches—old and new— are exclusive by nature. They don't mean to be, but they are by necessity.

Once a congregation has decided to meet at a set time, in a specific place, with a particular style, and with a certain agenda, though it will attract some people, it is bound to exclude many others.

It will exclude all those who:

- for family, work, and other reasons cannot attend at that time
- live too far away to get to the place
- are put off by the style of the gathering (such as the music), or
- don't identify with the congregation's agenda (to worship Christ).

This is a huge problem for Christians because we worship an all-embracing God, who died on the cross with his arms outstretched in a welcome to everyone. The *exclusive* manner of our worship contradicts the *inclusive* nature of the person we worship.

> THE *EXCLUSIVE* MANNER OF
> OUR WORSHIP CONTRADICTS
> THE INCLUSIVE NATURE OF
> THE PERSON WE WORSHIP.

The only solution—a big claim!—is to start new Christian communities among people who find the existing church inaccessible, and introduce new believers to the wider Christian family.

The compass we've described will help you to do this. Follow the four values—missional, contextual, formational, and ecclesial—and you'll connect with people your Sunday congregation naturally leaves out.

For example, in downtown Ocala, Florida, Tattoo Parlor Church emerged among the clients and friends of a young artist named Nick. It is:

- *Missional.* Most who gather don't go to church.
- *Contextual.* Activities, worship, etc. are shaped by what the people are into.
- *Formational.* Gradually, those who attend are being formed in the Christian faith.
- *Ecclesial.* Not many churches would have welcomed Nick with his head, face, and neck covered in tattoos, nor his friends. So right where they are, they have become a new Christian community for folks like them. Their challenge now is to grow links with the wider church.

These four values reflect some of the great doctrines of the Christian faith:

- the mission of God (God inhabits the world in generous love)
- the incarnation (God enfleshed in human culture)
- the Great Commission (God calls his followers to make disciples)
- the church's inclusiveness (God connects all people together across space and time or "catholicity").

Together, these values are one way of telling the Christian story. The missional God goes out to the world in love. He became a human being in Jesus, who offered salvation in a way people around him could understand. Jesus gathered a community to form disciples across the globe. His followers do this by multiplying Christian communities that enrich people's everyday worlds.

Use the compass and you will live this story.

As you do so, your discipleship will be given a eucharistic hue. The Eucharist is the central Christian meal in which we are re-membered as a body together into the life, death, resurrection, and coming again of Jesus. The basics of the Eucharist include four actions: take, bless, break, give (Mark 14:22). You and your friends will be called by God ("taken"), and will be supported in prayer ("blessed"). You'll go out from an existing congregation ("break"), and the Holy Spirit will offer you as the body of Christ to folks outside the church ("give").

People will gather around, hear the word, receive the gift, consume it, be transformed into a new Christian community, and be sent out to repeat the process. Communal life with Jesus will be passed from one generation to the next, and from one context to another.

CHAPTER 3
A Map

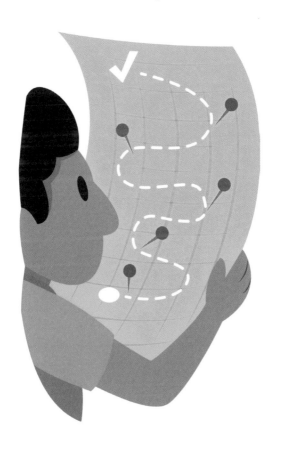

The second item you need for 21st century discipleship is a map. A compass points you in the right direction, but a map shows you the route to take. You need both compass and map to get to your intended destination—otherwise you will simply wander.

A group of Christians started a church focused on young people. They hung out after school with them, had 101 ideas before breakfast for what to do, but felt they were not making progress.

A senior church leader asked them to draw what they were trying to achieve. Their diagram was a bit like the *loving-first cycle* on the next page. They were seeking to:

- connect with the young people
- build community with them
- share Jesus, and
- start a worshipping congregation.

When they mapped it, they spotted a huge gap between building community and starting a congregation. They needed to put in some smaller steps, which would include weekend events to share Jesus. Without looking at the map, they wouldn't have noticed this gap.

The loving-first cycle

The "map" below describes how most new Christian communities seem to emerge. We call it *The loving-first cycle*. It's a way of thinking that will help you plan your journey, recognize how far you've travelled, and decide where to go next.

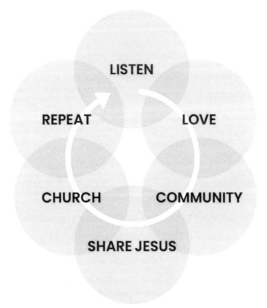

LISTEN

REPEAT

LOVE

CHURCH

COMMUNITY

SHARE JESUS

Like any map, you can choose from a variety of routes. But they all have these features in common:

- You *listen* lovingly to God and to people around you.
- Through listening, you prayerfully discover a simple way to *love* these people.
- You build *community* with them in the process.
- As trust deepens, you find natural opportunities to *share Jesus*, as part of a richer life.
- A new Christian community with the character of *church* takes shape among those coming to faith, where they are.
- New believers *repeat* the journey in their own way.

Of course, life is messier than a diagram! So the circles may overlap, pile on top of each other, or happen in a different order. Sometimes teams go back and refocus on an earlier circle. But we've found that generally, new communities follow this cycle, however loosely.

Each circle continues when you add the next. So you keep "listening" and "loving," for example, as you move on to "community." As you do so, you may decide to adapt what you are doing. Perhaps your "listening" suggests that you could do whatever you have started in a better way.

This cycle is not a theoretical idea. It is what we have observed more and more Christians doing across the globe. They know the gap between the world and the current church is too big for their friends and contacts to leap across. So they are following this cycle to start new Christian communities.

Listening comes first and guides the whole journey.

The important thing is that "listening" comes first and guides the whole journey. Below are some examples of groups who started through the act of listening.

Thirst

Sue got to know fellow parents at the entrance gate to the school. She "listened" to them and discovered that many would like to hang out together.

So, as an expression of "love," she arranged for them to meet on Thursday mornings in the school staff room. She provided coffee, fruit juice, and croissants. The parents watched a video about life issues from a gentle Christian perspective and shared their reactions.

In time, Sue noticed that some were becoming interested in Christ. So she "shared Jesus" by starting a Tuesday morning exploratory Bible study. Meanwhile, the Thursday get-togethers continued.

Gradually the Tuesday group learned how to pray and began simple worship. Sue would light a candle, play some Christian music, discuss a Bible passage, and invite topics for silent or spoken prayer.

She suggested people bring a postcard or picture to inform their prayers. Or if someone enjoyed photography, they could take photos to illustrate prayer themes.

Members of the Tuesday group became enthusiastic as "church" took shape among them. "This is brilliant for us!" they exclaimed. "But it's no good for our children at school, nor for our partners at work, nor for many of our friends. Can't we do something with them?"

So they did. They "repeated" the cycle by starting a gathering on Saturday afternoons with all-age activities, food, and some Christian input. The original group, *Thirst*, had spawned *Thirst too.*

Hot Chocolate

Hot Chocolate began in Dundee, Scotland, when a group of Christians took mugs of hot chocolate to teenagers hanging out in the city center.

Over the chocolate, the churchgoers "listened" to the young people and discovered that they wanted a place to rehearse their band. As a statement of "love," they got permission for the band to practice inside the nearby church, and for the young people to decorate and use a room in the basement.

"Community" formed as the young people gathered in their room, supported by the Christian volunteers.

When the teenagers began to ask spiritual questions, the volunteers replied, "We meet regularly to eat together, have fun, do some planning and praying, and discuss our Christian faith. Why don't you visit us and see what we do?"

A trickle of young people took up the invitation. The churchgoers had to adapt their planning meeting so the teenagers felt at home, but they were able to create a welcoming atmosphere as they invited these newcomers in. This was how they "shared Jesus."

Over time, this worshipping heart of the community has developed into "church" for the teenagers involved.

11 Alive

Tim, a minister in Britain's East Midlands, was frustrated that no young families were attending his church. So he spent some time "listening" to them, and with a few others in the church he started *11 Alive*.

After the Sunday service, the back of the church was set up cafe-style. Families gathered, played board games, chatted, enjoyed simple refreshments, and some of the adults read the newspapers. This was the church practicing "love."

"Community" formed as families attended regularly. A short act of worship at the end became an acceptable way to "share Jesus."

Every eight weeks, the community ate together. Afterwards, people formed four teams. Each team prepared two acts of short, accessible worship, so that all the worship was organized for the next eight weeks.

Each team was led by a churchgoer, but any member of the community could take part. Atheists and agnostics helped to plan the worship and sometimes lead it. They might introduce a song, read a poem, say a short prayer, or interview someone as part of the talk.

"It greatly accelerates their journey to faith," Tim remarked. When, later, he was asked how many atheists and agnostics were involved, he replied, "Not many at the moment. That's because most have come to faith."

Messy Church

Messy Church is a way of being church for families and others. It's Christ-centered, for all ages, based on creativity, hospitality and celebration. It began with a group of Christians in Portsmouth (UK) listening and asking, "How best can we love families in our community?"

They listened to what people wanted for their families and, using those requests, provided a format that included "love" (an accessible day of the week and time of day, a warm welcome, uncritical acceptance of difficult behavior, high quality hands-on activities and a sit-down meal), "community" (in intentional hospitality at every activity table and at the meal table) and "share Jesus" (through each activity and through a gathered celebration with a short story, song, and prayer).

The generosity and warmth of the Messy Church experience, the friendship groups who arrive together and the mix of ages provide instant easy "community." The Bible focus of every activity makes it straightforward to "share Jesus" on a micro level as people make things together and on a larger scale through the gathered celebration, singing songs, and praying prayers with language and liturgy that gently expand the worship experience.

Over time, the (necessarily large) team may grow in discipleship themselves as they plan each complex and demanding session together, encountering God's word, experiencing prayer, working through conflict. They may also draw Messy family members onto the team, where they too grow in faith. Or they might concentrate on a small group of interested people, like younger leaders or those passionate about social action, and spend time and energy helping them take further steps together towards Jesus in these spheres of interest. Discipleship happens mainly through friendships, modeling faith practices and doing life alongside people of all ages.

When leaders move away from their original church, they often "repeat" by starting a new Messy Church in their new neighborhood, based on their previous experience.

Rounded mission

Sometimes people wonder how to travel from the first three circles of the cycle to the next three. The stories we have just told illustrate how this can happen.

- *Thirst* did so by starting a second group, at a different time of the week, with people who wanted to explore Christianity.
- *Hot Chocolate* invited enquirers to the volunteers' planning meeting and sculpted the evening around those who came.
- *11 Alive* encouraged the whole group to journey together with a pattern that allowed individuals to travel at their own pace. *Messy Church* does something similar.

In all these examples, each of the circles continued as teams focus on the next. The leaders kept "listening" as they began to concentrate on another part of the cycle. The same was true of the other circles.

This is important because each circle displays an aspect of God's kingdom:

- *Listening* shows respect, which is a kingdom quality. It affirms the other person by valuing their contribution (Acts 11:12).
- *Love* can take the form of pastoral care. For example, environmental concern (love for creation), or promoting social justice (love for marginalized persons) are kingdom traits (Matt. 25:40).
- *Community* is integral to the kingdom. Human beings were created to live in loving relationship with God and each other (Lk. 10:25-28). We were created for community.

We were created for community.

- *Sharing Jesus* is having conversations about the person who announced the kingdom (Mark 1:15).
- *Church* and the kingdom will become one when Jesus returns (Rev. 21:1-2).
- *Repeat* witnesses to the expansive nature of the kingdom, which is like a seed that grows into a vast tree (Matt. 13:31–32).

Thus one circle is not a mere stepping stone to another, to be forgotten when you move on. Each circle has kingdom value that will continue to benefit the initiative as you move to the next phase.

If you don't travel through all the circles, don't despair! Each step has its own intrinsic worth. You introduce each circle as an end in itself, not as a means to reach the next stage. Listening well has its own value, as does loving, building community, sharing Jesus, and so on. Not everything your team starts will move into becoming "church"; in fact much will not, and that's okay. Each step further unleashes beauty, truth, and goodness in the world.

What's more, the Great Commandment (to love others Jn. 13:34) and the Great Commission (to make disciples Matt. 28:18-20) are brought together in a single, integrated initiative. The team moves from gathering people around its action(s) of love to sharing the gospel and helping new believers grow in their faith.

> **THE TEAM MOVES FROM GATHERING PEOPLE AROUND ITS ACTION(S) OF LOVE TO SHARING THE GOSPEL AND HELPING NEW BELIEVERS GROW IN THEIR FAITH.**

To form a comprehensive picture of the Great Commandment and the Great Commission, the Anglican Communion and Britain's Methodist Church increasingly use The Five Marks of Mission.

The loving-first cycle resonates with these five marks:

- *Tell* others about Jesus
- *Teach* and baptize them in the faith
- *Tend* to people's pastoral needs
- *Transform* the unjust structures of society, and
- *Treasure* the natural world.

The cycle includes and extends these, and joins them into a process. Whereas the five marks list the ingredients of integrated mission, the loving-first cycle offers a route for getting there.

Rather than the different dimensions of the kingdom flourishing after a new congregation has emerged, they are present in its birth, right from the beginning.

Use the map!

Here's a tool that can help you follow Jesus in a 21st century way: look at where you are on the cycle.

Ask whether God is calling you to the next circle, or whether he wants you to stay where you are, or refocus on a previous one and do it better.

Then consider what concrete steps you should take—either to improve an existing circle or to move on.

Keep pressing to the end of the cycle, always in prayer and always in consultation with others in the community.

This acronym, *EARS*, may help you:

Explore as a team what you should do next.

Ask everyone, "Is it a good idea?"

Respond to what you hear.

Spoil yourselves when you've held your "response" meeting. Give yourselves a treat!

CHAPTER 4
Food for the Journey

On any lengthy journey, you need to take some food. Nourishment is so vital that we can easily take it for granted. But ignore food on a long journey with children, and they will loudly remind you! Our Christian discipleship needs food as well—not just food for ourselves, but food to share with others on the way.

So, after finding one or more friends in a corner of your life and discovering a simple means to love the people around you, remember, as you befriend them, to share your feelings and thoughts about Jesus as opportunities arise.

Worried about this last step? There's no need. It's as simple as telling a friend where to find a bargain. If you heard about a great offer and you knew your friend would like it too, you wouldn't keep the news to yourself. You'd share it.

It's the same with Jesus. He has a great offer for people who want a fuller life (Jn. 10:10). So, why wouldn't you tell people who are gathering around your organized love?

Remember: you and your friends are not loving people just to get them into faith. That would smack of manipulation. Your love is unconditional—you will go on loving people in your community whether they respond to the gospel or not.

Sharing your experience of Jesus with those who are interested is part of your love. He is good news for you, and he might be good news for them. If they are uninterested, that won't make any difference to your love for them. Your love will continue regardless.

Go on loving people in your community whether they respond to the gospel or not.

You can share Jesus without pressuring people or feeling awkward. It can be as comfortable as enjoying a meal. You'll be sharing food "from heaven" that will nourish your team as well as people wanting a richer life (Jn. 6:32).

Here's how it could work.

An invitation

Imagine Lisa teams up with Malik. They give free croissants and coffee to their work colleagues each Monday morning. This provokes conversations and strengthens office relationships.

When asked why they do this, they say something like, "We're into practical spirituality, and this is what we do."

If pressed, they add, "If you want to know more, we meet after work on Tuesdays and for half an hour we explore spirituality. Jesus is known as one of the world's greatest spiritual teachers. We look at stories he told and discuss them. Why don't you visit and see what we do?"

Sharing thoughts, feelings, and experiences

Say Josh, a coworker of Lisa and Malik, accepts the invitation. Someone from the group explains that they dwell in one biblical story over several weeks. "We let it seep into our lives and see what happens."

The group reads the story and asks, "If this story happened today, what would it look like?" They have fun reimagining the story in their context.

At the end, a short "head space" allows them to pray to God as they understand the divine at that point, or share positive thoughts for others.

Next time they re-read the story, recap their previous discussion, and ask, "What is this story saying to me? What am I getting out of it?"

In the third session they discuss, "Could this story make a difference to my life? If so, how?"

Someone explains, "We've said we're into practical spirituality. So we see if the story does make a difference and report back next time. It's an experiment. So, by definition it may work or it may not. Either way, let's share what happened when we meet again."

At the next meeting, they share their experiences by asking, "Did the story make a difference? How?"

These four enjoyable *Discovery Bible Study* questions (available in the *FX Godsend* and *FX Connect* apps) are a welcoming way to explore spirituality from a Jesus perspective:

- If this story happened today, what would it look like?
- What is this story saying to me?
- Could the story make a difference to my life? If so, how?
- Did this story make a difference to my life? If so, how?

Josh can readily join in. And so can Christians who are anxious about sharing their faith. They simply answer the questions: "How did the story make a difference to my life?" It's as easy as a book club, or a conversation about a film, or a family discussion.

Alternative approaches

This is not the only approach, of course. For example, you could adopt a "Bite, Chew, Savor, and Digest" approach, using *Lectio Divina* (a traditional practice of Scripture reading):

- What word or phrase in the story stands out for me? ("Bite")
- What is it saying to me? ("Chew")
- If God exists, what would I want to say to him in response? ("Savoring" a meal often includes commenting on it.)
- How can I be a better gift to others and creation as a result of pondering this story? ("Digest")

Or you could ask these *kingdom* questions:

- What's the story saying that would bring a fuller life to the world?
- Where can we see signs of this fuller life around us?
- What could we do individually or as a group to increase these examples?
- In the next session: what have we done and what were the results?

Or you could invite people to *wonder* about the story:

- I wonder what it was like? I wonder if the sun was shining? What was she wearing? In what tone of voice did he speak?
- I wonder what the story is saying to me or to us?
- I wonder what I (or we) might do in response?
- In the next session: I wonder where God was in what I (or we) tried to do?

Or you could use these *Deep Talk* questions:

- What do you like about the story?
- Where are you in the story?
- What would you change in the story?

You can even mix-'n-match these questions, adapt them, or make up your own.

A group of millennials used the *Discovery Bible Study* approach, but they were impatient with the first two questions: "If this story happened today, what would it look like?" and "What is it saying to me?" They went straight to the third question, "How could the story make a difference to my life?"

The approach was used flexibly. Remember the "compass" value, "be contextual"? This is a good example. They did what worked for the group.

However, sometimes people say, "We use *Discovery Bible Study,* but have different questions." For example, "What does the story say about God?" "What does it say about humanity?"

This is not the same approach. These are cognitive questions, not experiential ones. They put the emphasis on knowledge rather than practice, on thinking rather than imagining. And they can make people new to the story anxious about getting the right answer.

Our advice is to use questions that . . .

- don't have right and wrong answers
- invite people to explore
- are less about belief and more about people's experience of their beliefs
- encourage people to share, and
- focus on application to life.

Dinner Church

Dinner churches are springing up across the United States and have their equivalents in other countries as well. This is a form of church centered around a shared meal, as practiced by the 1st century church (Acts 2:46). The meal is a sign of God's extravagant grace, a banquet of love to which all are invited regardless of their socioeconomic status (1 Cor. 11:17-26).

Imagine some Christians help with a food pantry and give free food to people experiencing poverty. Eventually, they start dinner church for clients of the pantry.

People gather one evening a week, eat together, and socialize. Someone offers a short Christian talk, referred to in dinner church culture as a "Jesus story."

But what if rather than the talk, your team decided to do a version of *Discovery Bible Study*? Either read a gospel story or show a cartoon version. (For one example, go to "Jesus Washes His Disciples Feet" at https://www.youtube.com/watch?v=bv5ajWNrnt4). Then invite people, in their table groups, to discuss one or more of the discovery questions.

This would:

- Make dinner church easier. There's no need to prepare a talk as discussion happens instead.
- Save leaders time. Preparation only requires deciding on the next story.

- Encourage more engagement. Instead of minds wandering during the talk, guests engage immediately in discussion.
- Put the Bible at the center of dinner church. Focus shifts from the person presenting to the gospel story.

Of course, there is no either/or here. Sometimes you could have a talk, and other times you could do *Discovery Bible Study*.

Then, gradually and with the group's consent, you could build on the discussion to introduce a richer diet of worship. For example:

- You might include a time of reflection, with a lighted candle on each table and some background Christian music.
- You might encourage spoken prayer by asking people to write a prayer or bring one to share with others.
- If you introduce Christian songs and hymns, you don't need a worship band from an existing congregation. The group may come to depend on the band and struggle if the volunteers stop being available. Why not start simple, with an iPad for instance? In time, invite community members to choose the

songs and be responsible for downloading them. The community will be trusting the Spirit to work through the resources within it. Maybe some musicians from within the community will eventually lead worship.

- Look for gifts within the group that can be utilized creatively in worship. For instance, someone with an artistic eye might bring an object or painting to spark prayer, or a writer might bring a poem to read aloud that the group can reflect on together.

- Look through a service of Holy Communion. What ingredients are absent from the community's worship? Take one of them—confession, for example. Do some research on why churches have included confession in their worship, and then look up some examples of confession in worship.[5] Share what you have learned and ask the community, "What forms of confession might work for us?" Encourage members of the community to come up with their own ideas. Try one or two for a while.

....

5. Search for "why confess sins in worship", "ideas for confessing sin in worship", "prayers of confession".

When the energy evaporates, pause the "confession spot" and repeat the process with a different ingredient, such as the creed or the blessing. By doing this, the community will be authoring its own worship style.

Adapt one or two of these ideas, and you will grow a community of worship producers rather than consumers. People will be contributing and sharing their gifts, rather like the congregation in 1 Corinthians 14:26–33.

Addressing your fears

Maybe you like the Bible-discussion approach, but you're worried that someone will ask a question and you won't be able to answer it, or that they will find good counter-arguments to your reply, and you'll look foolish.

Here's a possibility: You don't *have* to answer people's questions! Indeed, it may help them if you don't.

Say someone asks a factual question and you're not sure how to respond. Invite the group to Google it. (After all, this is a 21st century way of following Jesus!) You can discuss which sites are reliable sites to visit. After checking with Google, look it up in the Bible together.

When someone asks a question of opinion, reply: "From what we know about Jesus so far, what do we think he would say?"

Suggest people prayerfully (or thoughtfully) consider their responses and share what comes to them. Encourage people to listen to, rather than correct, each other.

Remind them that the church is full of different views, and this variety offers a broader glimpse of God. Make it easy for people not to contribute if they prefer to just listen.

If the issue is difficult or provocative, you might prepare the group in advance: "When we've shared our reactions, we'll have another brief silence. Then we'll take turns, if we wish, to say where we've seen God-like love in people's responses—someone's smile, another person's careful listening, what someone else said."

After alternative opinions have been heard, the discussion can move on. Differences have been honestly faced, everyone has been heard, no one has been judged, World War III has not broken out, and you've avoided looking stupid.

Remember: our eternal destiny does not depend on getting the "right" answers. After all, for 1800 years or more the church got the wrong answer about slavery. If our place in heaven depends on having right answers, St. Augustine, Martin Luther, John Calvin, and many other Christian heroes will not be there!

Clearly that's absurd. We are saved by grace, not by right answers. So don't worry if people come up with the "wrong" response. Focus instead on the vital spiritual habit of taking one's bearings from Christ.

We are saved by grace, not by right answers.

Keep asking, "From what you know about Jesus so far, what do you think he would say?" and you will teach people to ground their thoughts on him. You'll help them to change the soundtrack in their minds.

Leadership is about helping other people to see what you can see. As former Church of England archbishop Rowan Williams once said, "this does rather presume you get out of the way first." So walk alongside people as they explore Christ. Don't be in front and obscure the view!

Growing to maturity

Going back to our earlier fictional story, as soon as possible, ask newcomer Josh to lead the discussion. Give him the story. He knows the questions. All he needs to do is to watch the time, keep the group on task, and invite people to talk—time, task, talk.

When people in the group grow in Christ and need more "solid food," point one person in advance to a podcast perhaps with background information about the story, and another to maybe a YouTube video applying the story to life. (Don't forget to use recognized Christian authorities.) Again, this is 21st century discipleship!

The two people can share what they've learned before the discussion starts. The group is now accessing wisdom from the church at large.

In this way, members will come to rely on the Spirit working through:

- Scripture
- the group
- experience, and
- the wider body.

Of course, it doesn't stop there. Discussion-based Bible study is not the only way for people to grow in the faith. New Christians and those exploring will also benefit from more formal instruction within the community—by the leader, a local minister, a

YouTube video, or a live-streamed sermon—in the context of deepening worship.

There will be room, too, for short courses organized by the local church covering Bible, ethics and doctrine, and opportunities in the wider church such as conferences, prayer retreats, and much else.

> **SIMPLE DOES NOT EQUAL GOSPEL-LITE, IT JUST MAKES THE GOSPEL MORE SHAREABLE AND ACCESSIBLE.**

Keep the structure simple. Simple does not equal Gospel-lite, it just makes the Gospel more shareable and accessible. Consider the following list:

- *Anyone* can lead these Bible discussions. It's every member ministry (1 Pet. 2:9).
- Enquirers can easily join in (Acts 8:26-40).
- Scripture does the evangelism and disciple making (Rom. 10:17).
- Christians share their faith almost without knowing (Matt. 25:37-38).
- Seekers see how the Bible and the Christian community impact life (Jn. 8:30).

- Leadership is shared with newcomers, increasing their commitment to the group (Jn. 4:29).
- New Christians learn how to study the Bible, apply it to their lives, share it with their friends, and find helpful resources (Jn. 4:39-42).
- If the leader moves on, the group has the means to keep going—sustainability is built in (1 Thess. 2:17).

Everybody can feel at home. No Christian knowledge is assumed, different views are listened to, anyone can take part, power is given to the group, and above all, space is left for the Holy Spirit. Even not-yet Christians who are exploring faith could start a group like this!

If your team wants to follow Jesus in a 21st century manner, *Discovery Bible Study* (and the alternatives we've mentioned) is a simple and effective approach. It will nourish the team's spiritual life and give members the experience to help enquirers. It is your packed lunch to be shared with others.

CHAPTER 5

The Address of Your Destination

GPS is now a common tool in travelling, but it works best when you have an address as your destination. So, to follow Jesus in a 21st century way, it helps to have not only a compass, a map, and some food, but also the address of where you're going. The *FX Godsend* and *FX Connect* apps describe the address of that destination in the language of Fresh Expressions of Church as:

"New Christian community,
Growing in four overlapping sets of relationships,
All founded on Jesus."[6]

The four relationships are:

- With God directly in prayer, worship, and study.
- With the outside world.
- With the wider church.
- Within the new community itself.

This is the essence of the church: four overlapping sets of relationships, all rooted in Christ.

6. Mike Moynagh, "How to . . . Start a 'Fresh Expression'" (Stoke Gifford, Bristol: Diocese of Bristol, Fresh Expressions Material) <https://www.bristol.anglican.org/howto>. Accessed 2020. http://www.bristol.anglican.org/content/pages/documents/d9623c6d3210d3b7c9a944b7fed45f9b14845b95.pdf

> **THIS IS THE ESSENCE OF THE CHURCH: FOUR OVERLAPPING SETS OF RELATIONSHIPS, ALL ROOTED IN CHRIST.**

Take the church at Corinth, for example:

- It experienced God directly (1 Cor. 12:7–11).
- It engaged with the outside world (1 Cor. 14:23–25).
- It connected to other Christian communities: members read Paul's letters, looked up to people in the wider church (1 Cor. 1:12), and provided financial support to other parts of the body (2 Cor. 8:10).
- Members interacted relationally in worship (1 Cor. 14:26–31).

These four sets of relationships are equally important because Jesus is central to each, and together they comprise a balanced and healthy community. They make the church unique; no other institution or community combines these four particular sets of relationships.

The relationships have been expressed in myriad ways, and the one Spirit has worked through this variety. So if you start a new Christian community and it looks rather novel, don't worry! It can still be an authentic expression of the people of God. Just look for ways to deepen these four sets of relationships.

Surely there must be more to church

What about Scripture, the sacraments, leadership, and discipline (i.e. "rules," such as who can take Holy Communion)? Are they not fundamental to the church?

One way to answer this is to distinguish between the *essence* of the church and what is *essential* for the church. The two need not be the same.[7]

Umpires are essential for baseball, but are not the essence of the game. A legal document is essential to be married, but is not the essence of the relationship. In many cultures a knife and fork are essential for eating, but are not the essence of the meal.

The four overlapping sets of relationships are the essence of the church, while Scripture, sacraments, recognized leadership, and at least

---

7. This is rather different from the distinction theologians normally make between the *esse* (the essence) of the church and the *bene esse* (the well-being) of the church.

some rules (generously applied) are essential for the church.

The essentials originated in the church's relationships—from within the community Jesus founded. And the Holy Spirit works through them now to build up the church's relationships with God directly, the world, the wider church, and within the community itself.

Non-sacramental forms of worship, social events, outreach activities, organizational arrangements, and so on all have a similar purpose.

This means that all the practices of the church must serve the church's four sets of relationships—harkening back to the *contextual* point of the compass.

What has worked for you may not work well for your community. You may have to study Scripture, worship, exercise leadership, and evolve rules and practices that are different than what you are used to. When that happens, you are being contextual.

Remember Tim in Chapter 3? As the church's leader, he initiated "11 Alive," in which agnostics and atheists came to faith by helping with the worship. People belonged before they believed.

Tim said, "I love preaching and leading worship. But I have been up front only once in the past three years. I sit alongside everyone else. The community has had to teach me how to be a pastor among them."

Here then is the answer to a question many people ask: "What can change, and what must stay the same?"

Remember the essentials

What must stay the same is the existence of the four overlapping sets of relationships that comprise the church—with God directly, with the world, with the wider church, and within the community. No community can call itself "church" if it lacks one or more of these relationships.

Everything else can change, and often should, so long as the church remains true to its fundamental nature, which is these four sets of relationships centered on Christ. The key test of what comprises the church is the existence and strengthening of these relationships.

Imagine a new community meets on Thursday evenings:

- Members study Scripture in the context of worship and prayer. They discover that the early Christians met on the first day of the week and wonder if they should do the same.

- But how would this affect their witness in the world? They realize that in their context Sunday worship would not work. Too many people are on shift work, perhaps.
- They then ask what other Christians do. (They pay attention to the wider church.) They discover that many Catholic churches hold Mass on Saturday evenings and that in Muslim-majority countries Christians often worship on Fridays. Christians have not always gathered only on Sunday.
- Through discussion within the fellowship, they decide to continue worshipping on Thursday evenings, but to include prayer for those Christians who meet on Sundays. They will also make a special effort to meet on Easter Sunday.

The community has contextualized when it meets, but in a manner that seeks to do justice to the four sets of church relationships. In other words, these relationships help to discern God's will.

How can a new Christian community listen to the Spirit?

- By talking and listening to God in prayer, study, and worship.
- By conversing with others in the outside world in the missional context.
- By consulting the wider church, and continuing to listen even if the new community and wider church disagree.
- By sharing within the new community itself.

Through all these conversations, the promptings of the Spirit can be heard and tested, as happened at the Council of Jerusalem in Acts 15.

- There was "much discussion" (v. 7). Participants listened to one another.
- They listened to the missionary context as Paul and Barnabas described what had happened among the Gentiles (v. 12).
- James exposited Scripture (v. 13-21).
- Then they consulted the whole church in Jerusalem, and decided to send a letter (v. 22).

Conversing within these four sets of relationships is not always easy and doesn't guarantee agreement!

Even so, when Christians give new believers the tools to form and grow church, this practice of discernment is one of the most important to pass on. Engaging in life-giving conversations within the relationships that comprise the church will hold new believers within the family of God and nurture them in the historic faith.

Becoming church

This relational view of the church helps answer the question: when does a potential new Christian community become an actual expression of church?

We might say that a new Christian community is "on the way" to being church when its members start to grow into the four overlapping sets of relationships that make the church. Individuals are paddling in the shallow end of the church.

But as the community introduces the essential practices of the church—the word, access to the sacraments, recognized leadership, and necessary "rules" for the community to function—it begins to move toward the deeper end.[8]

When these essentials are present, the community has the "means of grace" for the Spirit to grow the relationships that define it as church. It can be recognized as an expression of the church—a worshipping community, a congregation, or a church in and of itself.

So, as you explore how to be a Christian community, perhaps with no off-the-peg guide for your context, keep asking: "Do our practices strengthen the four sets of relationships that comprise the church?"

Make sure Scripture, baptism and breaking bread, recognized leadership, and the rules of your community are present in an appropriate form. Surround them with other life-giving rhythms and habits. And check them against the yardstick: are they nourishing the community's four sets of relationships?

Prayerfully shape all you do to enable these relationships to flourish. That way, step by

Your new community will become more fully the people of God.

8. This picture of a swimming pool is taken from Clare Watkins and Bridget Shepherd's article, "The Challenge of 'Fresh Expressions' to Ecclesiology. Reflections on the Practice of Messy Church," *Ecclesial Practices*, 1, 2014, 92-110.

step, the ecclesial density of your community will increase. You will move from the shallow to the deeper end of the church. Your new community will become more fully the people of God.

Alphabet discipleship

Again, here is a 21st century form of discipleship.

- Find one or more friends in a passion of your life.
- Prayerfully discover a simple way to love the people around you.
- Grow your relationships with them.
- Share Christ, as part of a fuller life.
- Nurture a new Christian community among people coming to faith and connect them to the wider church.
- Then help them to focus *their* discipleship on starting further Christian communities.

To do this, you don't need a degree in theology, and you don't need countless years of Christian experience.

What you *do* prayerfully need is the Holy Spirit and your kit for the journey. The compass shows you the direction, the map helps you plan your route, food nourishes those who join you, and the address helps you to know when you have reached your destination.

Don't use the kit slavishly. Improvise, and your discipleship will be:

- *Action-based.* It will focus not on abstract knowledge (though this is important), but on practical love.
- *Beyond the church.* Your discipleship won't center on worship, small Christian groups, "another course," and sharing your gifts within the body, valuable though these are. You'll follow Jesus in the world, which is social holiness.
- *Communal.* You won't walk with Jesus on your own. You'll do so with one or more Christians, which is more fun.
- *Democratic.* You will show how almost any believer can start a new Christian community.
- *Easy* for anyone!

A, B, C, D, E—alphabet discipleship. The church will bubble up among people who find existing congregations inaccessible. You'll be a community, inebriated with love, for the people Sunday church leaves out.

CHAPTER 6
Finding Support

2 1st century discipleship: you can do it! But only with your eyes open. Jesus said that following him involves a cost (Matt. 16:24). The significant cost, perhaps, is the discomfort that comes from being vulnerable. When we put ourselves out there to start new things, failure and rejection can be part of the process. This is why a community of support is so important.

Bringing together your faith, God's mission, and the church also involves risk and uncertainty.

Bringing together your faith, God's mission, and the church will involve risk and uncertainty.

- *You may be unsure what to do,* how even to start. And once you've begun, success will not be guaranteed.
- *You may have to refocus your priorities,* perhaps even giving up other commitments. And you may not be sure in advance if it will be worth it.
- *You may have to abandon some of your ideas.* Maybe you have a plan for working with families, but listening to them shows that something else would work better.
- *You may have to leave behind some of your preferences*—about worship, for example. Paul Unsworth, a minister,

loved preaching. But in Kahaila Cafe's Wednesday evening worship, he found that atheists and agnostics engaged more deeply through discussion. So he had to give up that desire for the sake of the group.

- *You may have to be patient.* New Christian communities do not emerge overnight, and this may result in a lengthy period of uncertainty. You may wonder if you'll ever get to where you want to go.
- *You could burn out.* You could pour yourself into your initiative and become over-stretched and exhausted.

Face your vulnerability

This risk and uncertainty may leave you feeling a bit vulnerable. You may doubt that you could follow Jesus in a 21st century way. You may worry that it wouldn't work and you would be embarrassed. Deep down you may wonder if these doubts and fears mean there is something wrong with you.

If you feel like this, don't worry, it's natural. You are being invited to step into the unknown—to do something new for both you and the people you feel called to love.

Anything new makes most people feel at least a little exposed.

To find the courage to overcome these feelings, don't push them away. Uncomfortable feelings are like a child crying. If ignored, the child will cry even more. But give the baby a hug, and the child will quiet down.

So give your feelings a hug. Recognize them. If you can, amplify them in your mind, focus on them in prayer, and speak kindly to them. Spend time experiencing them. It's like paying attention to a crying child. In time the pain will subside.

Share how you feel with the friend(s) who've joined you in 21st century discipleship. Discuss the specific fears or feelings of inadequacy you each have. Be encouraged that you all feel vulnerable. Tell one another, "you're not alone."

You will feel worse if you think your worth as a person depends on the success of your initiative. So in your mind, separate who you are from what you do.

In Genesis 1:27–28 God made the first humans in his own image, and then he gave them the task of managing creation. The order is significant. First humans were made great, like God. Then they were given a great task.

First they were given their worth, then they were given a task to match their worth. Human worth comes *before* human activity. Our worth does not depend on what we do.

Keep saying this to yourself. "My worth does not depend on my achievements." Make sure you and your friends constantly remind each other of this. As you take each step along the way, remind yourselves that if it doesn't work, it doesn't matter. Your value as people does not depend on "succeeding." It rests on being made by God and loved by him.

Every time you feel anxious and doubt yourself, prayerfully remember: Your worth as a person is not at stake in 21st century discipleship. You already have value. God gave it to you at birth. You are worth so much that he died for you. Whatever happens, in his eyes you will remain intensely lovable.

Self-care

To sustain your discipleship, look after your spiritual health. Remember your private spiritual devotions. From time to time, attend a short prayer retreat or study day to recharge your batteries. You cannot give away what you do not have. If you want to offer others a growing relationship with Jesus, you must have an ever-deepening one with him yourself.

When you and your friend(s) meet, pray together, however briefly, using silent or spoken prayers. Periodically study a passage from Scripture. You could use one of the approaches described in Chapter 4.

Or each of you could study the passage on your own, and then share one reflection when you meet—a spur to keep up your personal devotions.

When your community starts to form, you and your team could immerse yourselves in the Pastoral Epistles—1 and 2 Timothy and Titus. They were addressed to first-century leaders of new Christian communities and remain a training manual for today.

Stay in touch with your original congregation, even if you've had to drop a church commitment to make time for your new community. Keep up with Christian friends and attend Sunday church whenever possible, perhaps once or twice a month. You will be grateful for the emotional and spiritual nourishment.

Starting and leading a new Christian community is a significant responsibility. "You can do it!" is more likely to be true if you recognize your limitations, seek advice, and make your own spiritual growth a priority.

> "YOU CAN DO IT!" IS MORE LIKELY TO BE TRUE IF YOU RECOGNIZE YOUR LIMITATIONS, SEEK ADVICE, AND MAKE YOUR OWN SPIRITUAL GROWTH A PRIORITY.

Keep asking, "Am I noticing areas where I need to deepen my discipleship, such as learning patience, growing in my ability to help other people discover and exercise their gifts, or becoming equipped to enable others to explore worship?"

Being on mission, with fellow Christians, in everyday life is the best way to mature in your faith. So make the most of the opportunities around you. Expand your skill base and grow in maturity as your community develops:

- Meet regularly with a wise Christian for spiritual support and mentoring.
- See if your church could help pay for you to attend the occasional conference, workshop, or course to assist your growth in spiritual and practical wisdom.
- If your initiative is under the wing of your local church, are you meeting regularly

with your minister or someone else nominated by the leaders? This should be a two-way accountability. You would be accountable to the church leaders for your initiative, and the leaders would be accountable to you for learning what God is doing in your community. Don't forget the principle, "Low control, high accountability."

- Consult "wise heads" and experts about safeguarding, health and safety, insurance, and so forth. Talk to people with relevant experience, such as teachers, if you are working with children or teenagers. Ask them, "If you were in my shoes, what would you do?"
- Above all, ask some friends, your original congregation or other Christians, such as another religious community, to pray regularly for your initiative. It's amazing how many leaders forget this! Prayer is your secret weapon.

Connect up

When you start a new Christian community, you offer to people outside the church a gift— the gift of communal life with Jesus.

Like any gift, this communal life must be offered appropriately. Just as it would make no sense to give a bottle of wine to a friend who's a teetotaler, it will make no sense to offer community with Christ in a manner that doesn't work for the potential recipients.

A gift also says something about the giver—about how she feels toward the other person, or about her character. "She would give that, wouldn't she!" So, when you offer communal life with Jesus, inevitably you will want your gift to reflect your understanding of what living with Christ involves.

And this is where some tension can arise, especially if you are acting in the name of your local church. As people come to faith, your church may expect them to worship and behave in a manner that reflects the church's tradition.

But you may find that aspects of the tradition don't work in this different context. Maybe people feel embarrassed by singing hymns, or some of the formal liturgy doesn't speak to them, or they can't sit still during a talk.

You may have to negotiate a way through the expectations of your church and those of your new community. There is no one right answer, except this: keep talking and listening to all involved.

If your church's leaders are puzzled by what is going on, why not invite one or two of them to your community? Or suggest they invite one or two members of your community to one of their meetings?

Maybe the leaders want to know why those coming to faith are not attending Sunday church or prefer a different style of worship to what they are used to. Let those new to the faith explain. Objections often melt away when people talk face to face.

Pray for win-win compromises that respect both the traditions of your church and the culture of the people in your new community.

For example, suppose your community wants to celebrate Holy Communion and you are not ordained, but your church expects an ordained minister to preside. There can be several ways through:

- You can hold an informal "remembrance of the Last Supper" or an agape meal without the presence of the minister. It would be important to say that this is not Holy Communion as your denomination or church understands it. You could see this as a step toward fuller sacramental worship, and pray that in the meantime "eucharistic grace" will extend from the worship of the original congregation to cover the new community.

- You can ask the minister to visit your community and preside at Communion. As a representative of the wider church, the minister will be a reminder that the community is part of a larger whole. Your minister might even consider becoming a "chaplain" to the community, providing pastoral and other support as time allows.
- Periodically you can hold joint services of Holy Communion with your parent church. Your team might even serve refreshments at the end. Instead of huddling together and feeling out of place, members would be involved and appreciated, and would meet people.

Some people talk about a "mixed economy" church: new and existing forms of church living alongside each other, with their distinctive missions, bound together by mutual love and respect.

But you could be more ambitious! Think "mixed church" or "blended ecology." Mix up the old and new in social, educational, and outreach events, and in shared worship where possible.

Instead of travelling on parallel tracks, might the old and the new one day merge together? The parent congregation would discover new ways of worshipping, and the new community would explore the riches of the Christian heritage. Gradually they would become more and more alike. It's begun to happen in some cases.

The wider church

If you are a leader in your denomination, diocese or network of churches, 21st century discipleship is both an opportunity and a responsibility. It could release a swarm of lay leaders who will need your help.

21st century discipleship is both an opportunity and a responsibility.

St George's in Deal, England, which has around fifteen new Christian communities, has seen over fifty new leaders. Many had not been in church leadership before. A minister named Chris said,

> "Interestingly, I think the ones who hadn't been in leadership were probably the ones who generated the best

communities, mostly because they gathered everyone and said 'Oh, help, what are we going to do now!' And everyone kind of got on board with it.'"[9]

These lay leaders need encouragement and support. Beyond what the local church can provide, the denomination, diocese, or network should invest in these leaders by:

- organizing study days and prayer retreats,
- funding formal learning on a spare or part-time basis, and
- offering advice on vocations. Starting a new Christian community frequently begins or accelerates a journey to ordination.

In particular, when teams start and develop new Christian communities on their own, they often become discouraged, lose their vision, or get stuck at an early stage of the "loving-first cycle" described in Chapter 3. Team members need:

---

9. Michael Moynagh, *Church in Life: Innovation, Mission and Ecclesiology* (London: SCM, 2017), 95.

- the accumulated wisdom of others who have travelled a similar journey,
- the wisdom of people with relevant expertise and life experience,
- the discipline of asking regularly, "What next?" and coming up with a plan, and
- the support of a community in which they are understood and affirmed.

In the business world, incubating entrepreneurs is a familiar concept, where budding entrepreneurs are given various types of support to help them succeed.

Denominations and dioceses are starting to do something similar for teams leading new Christian communities. Support is focused on the team, not just the leader, who may unexpectedly leave. If you support the leader, you cement fragility; if you support the team, you build in sustainability.

Support for new Christian communities, where it exists, has tended to be ad hoc, fragmented, and insufficiently connected to learning about good practice.

By contrast, the "incubators" now emerging offer systematic, integrated, and well-researched support. Described more fully in the next chapter, they make the promise "You can do it!" achievable.

CHAPTER 7
How to Start

So how might you begin?

- How might individuals start?
- How might local churches start?
- How might denominations, dioceses, or networks of churches start?

You may want to focus on the section in this chapter that is most relevant to you.

How might individuals start?

If you are a churchgoer, it is as simple as A, B, C, D.

- **A**sk a friend (or more). Form a team.
- **B**egin with what you've got. What in your life could you share with others?
- **C**hat about the possibilities with people in your context, and *listen* to their response.
- **D**iscover your next step.

Ask a friend

God works through communities—often tiny ones. He put Adam and Eve together to cultivate the garden. Jesus did ministry in a community of twelve disciples. When he sent his followers on mission in Luke 10, he sent them in pairs. Paul was part of a mission team, initially with Barnabas and John Mark, and then with others (Acts 13:1–5).

Don't try and start a new Christian community on your own. If Jesus and St. Paul believed in teams, why think you can do without one?

Begin with what you've got

Rather than trying to start from scratch, use the ingredients you already have. Start with:

- Who you are—your interests, passions, or whatever else makes life full for you.
- What you know—your expertise or knowledge of the context.
- Whom you know—friends, networks, and family.
- What you have—a home, car, and more.

Let's apply these questions to Louisa, for instance.

- Who was she? A community nurse, working from a medical practice.
- What did she know? That young mothers in her area had unusually high levels of post-natal depression.

- Whom did she know? Charlie and Charlotte, who lived near the families.
- What did they have? Charlie and Charlotte's front room, where the mothers could meet as a support group. Later the mothers explored spirituality and became a new Christian community.

Ask what God has given your small team. How could you share this with people around you?

If you're into film, for example, start a film club with people you know and their friends. Watch a film once a month. The next week meet over a meal to discuss it. Make it "a film club with a spiritual dimension." During the discussion ask, "If God exists, what would he think of the film?"

Chat and *listen*

Jesus listened. In his first recorded action (in Luke 2:46), he fired questions at the teachers in the temple and was absorbed by their answers. Throughout his public ministry, he kept asking people what they wanted and what they thought.

So, as you pray about what you might do, chat with people about your ideas, listen to their reactions, and ask for *their* ideas. Talk and listen:

- To God directly in prayer and Bible study.
- To the people you want to love. They are best placed to know if your idea will work, to help you, and to invite their friends.
- To others in the congregation and the wider church with wisdom to share. Why not Google who else is working with a similar demographic, or has started the type of thing you have in mind? Seek their advice. Ask friends to pray for you, and test your thoughts on them.
- To one another in the team.

This is "360 degree listening"—listening in the round—to *everyone* who might have something to contribute. When you listen, you dig the foundations of your initiative. The more you listen, the firmer your foundations.

When you listen, you dig the foundations of your initiative.

Listen with integrity. Be ready to change your mind. If the brilliant idea you've championed gets a lukewarm response, let it go. It will be worth it.

Sara Savage, a Cambridge University research psychologist, once said, "The experience of being listened to is so close to the experience of being loved as to be indistinguishable."[10] That's the great prize! The more you listen, the more you love.

Discover your next step

Prayerfully decide what God wants you to do next. The map from Chapter 3 will help you.

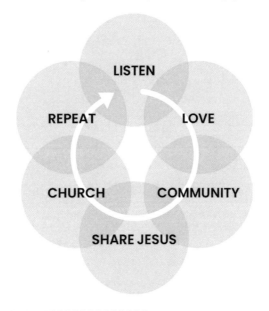

LISTEN

REPEAT

LOVE

CHURCH

COMMUNITY

SHARE JESUS

10. Michael Moynagh with Philip Harrold, *Church for Every Context: An Introduction to Theology and Practice* (London: SCM, 2012), 252.

Locate yourself on the cycle. Are you at the "listen" stage because you're starting out?

Or are you leading a well-established initiative, such as an evening meal for people experiencing homelessness? Did you listen to God and the context, organize your love, and then form relationships? If so you've reached the "community" stage.

Ask what steps would take you to the next circle. Might you evolve into "dinner church?" What steps would take you there?

Keep asking, "What will take us to the next stage?" Your next step might be to:

- *Stay where you are on the cycle and improve what you are doing.* Perhaps a "tea and muffin" group has reached the "community" circle. What step(s) would bolster community when the group meets?
- *Explore a step toward the next circle.* The team feels ready to "share Jesus" as part of a fuller life. What step might it explore? Themed conversations with a spiritual dimension?
- *Explore how to improve the step you're currently taking.* Perhaps you've introduced themed conversations, but some people don't engage. Instead of

the team selecting topics, try having the guests suggest them.

- *Explore a further step to build on the step(s) you're already taking.* Themed conversations have raised the spiritual temperature. Might you start a group with Discovery Bible Study at a separate time?

- *Return to an earlier circle.* You are at the "community" stage, but numbers are falling. Is "tea and muffin" the best way to love the people you have in mind? You might refocus on the "listen" stage. What would help you tune into those who don't come to "tea and muffin"?

The *EARS* framework, mentioned in Chapter 3, could help you plan the next step.

- *Explore as a team what you should do next.* Brainstorm possibilities and settle on your possible next step(s).

- *Ask everyone!* What do they think of your idea(s)? Vitally important, of course, are the people involved in your initiative. But don't overlook others, such as those who are praying for you, people with experience of a similar demographic, and people who've led an initiative like yours. And don't forget to ask God in prayer!

- *Respond to what you hear.* Discuss with your team members what you've heard and decide how to respond. For example:
  - » The idea isn't popular. The team rethinks and starts *EARS* again.
  - » The idea has been well received but needs modifying. Should the team use *EARS* to test the revised idea?
  - » The idea needs fleshing out. When? and How? for example. To test these details, *EARS* is repeated.
  - » The idea got the green light. The team maps the details and forges ahead.
- *Spoil yourselves when you've responded to what you've heard.* Once you've agreed on how to respond, enjoy a celebratory cake or some other reward. You're making progress. Even if your proposal got the thumbs down, you've learned what won't work and can put your energies elsewhere. This *is* a step forward, though it may feel disappointing. The team did some good asking and should celebrate a job well done.

Don't travel around "The loving-first cycle" unaided. For inspiration and advice, download the free *FX Godsend* app, or access the same material on the *FX Connect* app (the Fresh Expressions US version) or on the web (go to fxresourcing.org or FXGreenhouse.info).

FX Godsend will guide you through the cycle. It contains cartoons, stories, and practical wisdom for each stage, culled from different sources and representing years of experience.

Don't follow the advice slavishly. Use only what's helpful, adapt it, and supplement it with other resources. Let the material ignite your imagination and spark prayer.

How might a local church start?

If you're the church leader, again it's A, B, C, D:

- Assemble a core team to support you.
- Begin with who you've got.
- Create an incubator—sometimes called a studio or greenhouse—to support teams leading new Christian communities.
- Draw in others.

Assemble a core team

Find one or two people in the church who share your vision. Meet with them for prayer, support, encouragement, and advice. Expand the team when others show interest.

Don't worry if members are not part of the church's leadership. God often calls individuals who are on the edge of his people. David, overlooked by his family, became Israel's king. Jesus came from Galilee, an unfashionable region.

Explain to your fellow leaders that this is part of your calling. You are helping church members to live out their faith in the whirlwind of life.

In Chapter 1 we mentioned Wildwood United Methodist Church, which now has fourteen new Christian communities in a poor part of Florida. The journey started when Michael [Beck] recruited new blood to a slightly moribund Evangelism Committee.

Members were released from the demands of the existing congregation and given a single task: Do church with people who don't go to church.

Begin with who you've got

Michael's group started by prayerfully preparing a "people map"—a map of spaces where people gather to do life. It also mapped out "persons of peace" (Luke 10:6). These are individuals who open the door to their network or their practice, such as dog walking or tattooing.[11]

Then members offered to take one simple next step. For example:

- "I will hang out in the burrito joint on this day, at this time, just to pray for and connect with people in this space."
- "I used to be a tattoo artist. I know the owner of a tattoo parlor. I'll check if we can gather there and host spiritual conversations for those interested."
- "I like to run with friends. I'll make a Facebook page and invite people to join me."
- "I'll ask one or two people to help me make a list of people we can invite to our first prayer walk for racial peace."

Starting was that simple!

....

11. Michael Beck with Jorge Acevedo, *A Field Guide to Methodist Fresh Expressions* (Nashville, TN: Abingdon Press, 2020).

In your congregation, there may be people already involved in outreach. You might ask if they would like to add a further dimension.

A weekly luncheon club met at the back of a rural church. One Wednesday, the leaders brought a table into the main body of the church and put some lighted candles on it.

They invited those who wanted to stay behind after lunch to sit around the table, listen to some Christian music, hear a short story from Scripture, reflect silently, and listen to some spoken prayers—just fifteen minutes. There was no pressure. The luncheon club would continue as normal, whether or not people stayed behind.

Almost everyone took part. Add in a short discussion after the Scripture reading, and step-by-step this gathering had the potential to become a fuller expression of the church.

Could your church do something similar? Do you have a bereavement group, perhaps? Why not create a quiet space, with lighted candles, gentle music, and cards with Bible verses or other "sayings" for people to reflect on?

Think of initiatives that have travelled through the first three circles of "the loving-first cycle." Might they be ready to take a next step?

In addition, you could use the "Overview" in *FX Godsend* or the "FX Journey" in *FX Connect,* referred to above, to prepare a sermon series on 21st century discipleship. During the series, approach people who might have energy for this way of following Christ. "Energy for the kingdom" and "Holy Spirit" are two sides of the same coin.

At the end of the sermon series, invite those interested to meet for several weekday evenings. During the evenings, discuss the five "Overview" units in *FX Godsend* or *FX Connect.*

At the end, ask if anyone wants to try 21st century discipleship. Encourage them to find a friend or more, and in their teams to study the same "Overview" section.

Then invite the teams to meet together regularly—face-to-face or by video—for prayer, planning, and mutual support.

Create an incubator

In Wildwood, the Evangelism Committee morphed into a supportive community for leaders of "go teams" who catalyzed new Christian communities where life happens.

Leaders came together to imagine, create, and encourage each other.

In 2019 the group turned itself into an incubator, which it called a "studio." This is a community of missional imagination, involving whole teams who co-create new Christian communities, like artists slinging kingdom paint around.

Teams meet for prayer, learning, mutual support, and planning in particular. Every few months, they gather for a whole day. Each team plans one or more steps that will lead its community to the next stage of the loving-first cycle. Encouraged by the others, each team leaves with a plan.

Even if there is only one team, a church leader can start an incubator to nurture the new team. Other teams can be prayerfully invited to join when they are ready.

As in Wildwood, the incubator should include these vital ingredients:

- *A shared focus,* which is travelling through the loving-first cycle.
- *Just-in-time learning,* as teams use *FX Godsend* or *FX Connect* to get inspiration for how to move from one stage to the next. Teams discover what they need

to know, when they need it, and pray about it.

- *Regular gatherings,* in which teams come together to plan, share, learn, and pray. During the gathering, each team shares with other teams:

   What is? "What stage has our team reached on the loving-first cycle?"
   What could be? "What type of step are we ready to take next?"
   What will be? "Who in the team will do what, by when, over the next six months?"

- *A shared presence on social media,* so that teams can request prayer, exchange news, ask each other for advice, and thereby pool wisdom in the room. For example, a teacher on another team may have advice for an initiative among children.

- *Coaching/mentoring,* as and when teams need it, usually by Skype/Zoom.

Draw in others

When teams start to bear fruit, encourage them to share their experiences with others in the congregation.

Almost certainly members will ask, "When will the people being reached come to church?" The response to that might be, "We've asked them and they don't want to come."

Remind the congregation that every church is inaccessible to some because of when, where, how, and why it meets. Explain that the church is being made available to people who find it out of reach. Discuss other ways the original congregation can build connections with the emerging new Christian community.

As the story of a new community is told, in time other people may want to start something similar. If this is the case, you could hold another series of preparatory evenings, and invite those interested to join other teams in your incubator. Take those new teams through the *loving-first cycle*.

Before becoming a studio, the Wildwood "go teams" group went a step further than the confines of their own congregation. They reached out to Christians outside of their church. They worked with more affluent white believers on "the other side of the tracks" to challenge systemic racism.

They planned prayer walks for racial unity and weekend interracial revivals, and jointly started new Christian communities that crossed racial divides.

Wildwood was a struggling church on the edge of death, with few resources and a broken past. By drawing in others from the community they were able to experience a positive transformation. If they can start fourteen new Christian communities, gather the teams leading them into a studio for planning and mutual support, and use this collective energy to mobilize wider social change, *any* church can do something similar!

Feet first, not head first

You don't need lots of theory. You don't need years of training. You don't have to mobilize the church behind a big vision and raise tons of money. That would be a head-first approach.

Instead, begin with simple steps. Start with one or two "early adopters" and learn from their experience. Pray that their example spreads to others. Don't expect quick results. Every day pray for patience!

Of course, this is not the only way to start. But feet first, step-by-step has many benefits.

- You don't have to convince a lot of people of what you're doing.
- You don't have to solve all the problems first—you can address them as they arise and look for solutions in the experience of those involved.
- You don't need high-level skills in change management. Just start with a small group.
- You don't need everyone on board. Congregants can keep going as they are, if they want.
- You can encourage the new Christian communities as part of your pastoral work.

Network and denominational leaders

Leaders of a group of churches, a network, or a denomination wanting to encourage new Christian communities can start by appointing someone part-time or full-time to cultivate or enable them.

In 2014, the United Methodist Church in Florida appointed my co-author, Michael Beck, to this role, alongside his leadership of Wildwood UMC. Starting with his own

North Central District, five years later he was working with all eight.

He has found that A, B, C, D applies not only locally, but regionally too:

- **A**ssemble a guiding group to provide support.
- **B**egin with who you've got.
- **C**reate an incubator for teams starting new Christian communities.
- **D**raw in others.

Assemble a guiding group

Michael knew he couldn't go it alone in this denominational position or he would burn out. He wouldn't have enough resources. He would miss out on the contacts others in a team bring. And he would make poor decisions by relying on too narrow a range of experience.

So he began by drawing a group of people from different backgrounds to develop and champion the vision of multiplying new Christian communities within the denomination.

The group organized "Vision Days" to pollinate the concept with other churches. It identified hub churches with the potential to grow these communities. And it offered coaching to church leaders and individuals wanting to get involved.

Michael knew he could enlarge the group as time went on, so he just started with who was willing.

Begin with who you've got

The group sent out interest questionnaires to the eighty-seven churches in the district and started with those who responded with energy for the vision.

From this simple beginning, the district now has eighty new Christian communities alongside, and in fellowship with, the existing churches.

To supply a missing ingredient, the guiding group has become the nucleus of a studio for teams growing new communities across the district. The studio is providing a new focus for the work in the district.

UK experience suggests that cultivators (or in UK language "enablers") will follow something like this sequence of steps:

- Network with church leaders and others.
- Host an invitation day.
- Follow up with those interested.
- Invite them to a launch evening.
- Form an incubator of participating teams.

The initial *networking* will include church leaders and others who are likely to be enthused by the vision. They will be gatekeepers who point the cultivator to people starting new Christian communities, are intrigued by them, or already lead initiatives that have in effect travelled through the first three circles of the loving-first cycle and can move to the next stage.

Don't worry if only a few people are interested. The priority is to be focused. Concentrate on where the fire is, fan the flames, and eventually the blaze will spread.

The cultivator will meet with people who are interested, whether one-on-one or in planned question-and-answer groups.

The cultivator will then invite these and other contacts to an *invitation day*, where the idea of 21st century discipleship will be explained, and people will learn how to join an incubator.

Leaders wanting to be involved will need to do so with a team—"find one or more friends." Some may already have a team while others may have to gather one.

All that follows is based on teams, which is important. Support is not given to the leader alone, as this would reinforce fragility. If only the leader is supported and the leader moves on, the rest of the team will be left stranded. Instead, support is given to the team, which creates sustainability.

At this stage, it doesn't matter whether the team knows what it is going to do. It may be at the very beginning of *the loving-first cycle*, where it simply listens. The incubator will help teams get started, no matter how far along they are in the process.

As teams emerge, the cultivator may need some *follow-up conversations* to answer questions and clarify expectations.

Interested teams are then invited to a *launch evening*. They are introduced to the incubator concept and encouraged over the next couple of months to discuss the "Overview" units in *FX Godsend* or *FX Connect*.

They then bring what they have learned to a gathering, where the incubator is launched.

Create an incubator

From his experience in the North Central District of the Florida Methodist Conference, Michael is cultivating guiding groups in the other seven Florida districts. Now each of the eight districts throughout the state has a Fresh

Expressions team, which continue to cultivate these new Christian communities.

Starting with the North Central District guiding group, which will become the core of the first "studio," the intention is to multiply these "studios" across Florida, so as to realize the Bishop's vision of 500 new Christian communities by 2025. Similar incubators, known as "greenhouses," are being introduced in the Church of England and in other UK denominations.

Michael has found that teams leading new Christian communities need intensive support—the encouragement, motivation, stimulus, and learning made possible by joining up with other teams. By means of an incubator:

- Teams help each other to stay focused and keep travelling through the loving-first cycle.
- They hold one another accountable for being disciplined in planning. When teams are on their own, planning is often squeezed out by day-to-day demands. But when they meet with other teams, they share their plans and how well they worked. In this way they are able to learn

from the successes and failures of other teams and refine their own strategies.

- Teams pool their wisdom. There may be twenty to thirty people in the room who can offer advice among teams or point to other sources of help.

Just like a local church incubator, each incubator should comprise:

- *A shared focus,* progressing through *the loving-first cycle* as far as God takes you.
- *Just-in-time learning,* as teams use *FX Godsend* and *FX Connect* to travel from one stage of the cycle to the next. Teams discover what they need to know, when they need it, and pray about it.
- *Regular gatherings,* in which teams come together to plan, share, and learn. During the gathering, each team shares with the other teams:

    What is? "What stage have we reached on 'the loving-first cycle'?"
    What could be? "What type of step are we ready to take next?"
    What will be? "Who in the team will do what, by when over the next six months?"

- *A shared presence on social media,* so that teams can request prayer, exchange news, and ask each other for advice.
- *Coaching/mentoring,* as and when teams need it.

The regular gatherings need not always, or even mainly, be face-to-face. As we write, we know of several who are holding these gatherings by Zoom.

Each incubator should be led by a small team—maybe the cultivator and a couple of apprentices. This ensures continuity if the cultivator ever moves on.

It also increases capacity. The apprentices can use their experience to start further incubators, helping to multiply the number of teams in the denomination or network.

Draw in others

Once a studio has launched, Michael and his district guiding groups will continue to network and identify other teams wanting to grow new Christian communities. These teams will either be drawn into new studios, or be invited into an existing studio by means of:

- An invitation day.
- Follow-up conversations with those interested.
- A launch evening.

In all this, we still have much to learn. So perhaps our best advice is: don't be too zealous in following our advice!

Imagine . . .

It's fifty years ahead. Enabled by the Spirit, a galaxy of small Christian communities illuminates every corner of society. They love people around them, share Jesus to unlock a richer life, draw in new believers, connect them to the wider church, and see their contexts transformed.

This is church bottom-up—not the church descending on people, but the church growing organically around people's priorities in the textures of daily life.

> THIS IS CHURCH BOTTOM-UP: NOT THE CHURCH DESCENDING ON PEOPLE, BUT THE CHURCH GROWING ORGANICALLY AROUND PEOPLE'S PRIORITIES IN THE TEXTURES OF DAILY LIFE.

New believers are empowered to create their own contextually appropriate theologies. These are "local spiritualities" (like Adam's "classic car spirituality") that draw from the Christian heritage to address immediate concerns.

These spiritualities circulate, inspire other Christians, fuse together in some cases, and spawn further variants. Small-scale Christian love multiplies, resonates with people in contexts that matter to them, spreads meme-like along social networks, and begins to refashion society from the ground up. Thousands of Christian windows illuminate the social cathedral. Each small new Christian expression is like a uniquely colored pane of stained glass, shining together to paint the larger community in the technicolor love of God.

CHAPTER 8
Democratize
Church Planting!

f you are a church planter, this is an extra chapter for you. And we have good news for you—21st century discipleship will proliferate church plants faster than a conventional approach. When the whole people of God, the "priesthood of all believers" are released, every person can play a role. More groups of maturing disciples working together can multiply more Christian communities.

Traditional planting

Conventional church plants start with a team of perhaps twenty or so Christians. They host evangelistic and other outreach events. Through these, the team gathers enough people to launch a congregation of sometimes 100 or more. Further outreach helps the congregation to grow.

Large plants can reach a significant number of people, support a variety of Christian programs, and pay for ministry on a sustainable basis.

But what happens to the people the new church plant leaves out?

Imagine a neighborhood with young children, teenagers, busy commuters, second generation migrants, and people with mental health issues. The planting team can't serve them all. What can you do?

The solution? Start asking, "Whom are we not reaching?"

Keep that question on the agenda of your team meetings. Ask it in your prayer meetings. Bring it into the congregation's worship. Go on about it until people get cross with you. Then ask it again! Never stop.

The question will only matter to others if they know it matters to you. So refuse to be satisfied. Raise the bar of ambition. Keep asking, "Whom are we not reaching?"

Then introduce 21st century discipleship.

Democratizing church planting

You've planted at scale—now plant at the micro level. Introduce "every member mission"—church multiplication by everyone.

Teach members of your congregation to:

- prayerfully gather with one or more friends
- listen to God and their context
- find a simple way to love people around them
- deepen their relationships with them
- share the gospel appropriately as part of a fuller life

- form a new Christian community with those coming to faith and connect them to the wider church, and
- encourage new believers to repeat the process.

Any Christian can do this. For example, Caroline was a school teacher in Northwest London. She knew that some of her children's mothers had recently come from Sri Lanka and wanted to learn English. With a small team, she invited them to a weekly language cafe.

Up to twenty-five women sat around tables, had English afternoon tea, and discussed a topic in English. Some of the topics had a spiritual flavor, and after a while a few of the women met at a different time to explore Jesus. The language cafe continued as before.

For Caroline, this was not a new commitment unrelated to what else she was into. It added value to her existing life.

She didn't need to gather a large team, which can be difficult. She didn't need the skills and time that leading a big team require. She could start with an existing commitment and some friends. She was able to work with people who didn't go to church, by simply harnessing her own passions and relationships.

21st century discipleship magnifies a church plant's multiplying potential. You don't have to wait for a gifted leader to emerge or the money to come in to employ one, or for attendance to grow sufficiently to form a large team. Rather than delay before planting again, you can do so almost at once—with not just one plant, but lots!

From the beginning, you'll be connecting with people who are not coming to your new church and finding creative ways to reach them.

Never too small

You may ask, are niche congregations too small to bother with? In reality, some can be quite large. Indeed, if every congregation appeals to people who have something in common— because of when, where, how, and why it meets—even the largest congregation will be niche!

But imagine niche congregations arising all over the community with people for whom the traditional church is inaccessible. This is how the church can spill out into every microcosm of the community. This is following Jesus where life happens.

"Too-small" misses the point. The challenge is not size but reach. Whom is the congregation not embracing? And how might it draw close to people left out of the current church?

People with mental or physical disabilities, for example, or residents of an apartment block, or recent migrants from the same country may be served best by a smaller community in which:

- they can express themselves
- they can find Jesus alongside others with similar questions
- they can develop a Christian life that relates to their shared experiences, and
- they can contribute to the leadership.

Small may be just what they need. Remember: the kingdom of God is like a tiny mustard seed (Matt. 13:31–32).

In particular, the too-small argument outsources church planting to an elite. Only those who can gather a large group of people and get funding to secure a brick and mortar facility are considered "church planters."

What would have happened if Caroline had limited church planting to large teams that start large congregations? She never would have reached those Sri Lankan women.

Looking back, she said, "At the beginning I saw myself as a member of the church with gifts to contribute, but at the end I saw myself as a leader, able to start something new."

It was because church planting could be small and within her capabilities that she included it in her discipleship and discovered gifts she never thought she had.

Starting new Christian communities is not just for specialists.

Starting new Christian communities is not just for specialists. Democratize it! Make it the bedrock of following Jesus, see the church multiply faster than you ever imagined, and let the church become a welcoming home for everyone!

Best of both

Don't be an either-or person. Be both-and. Support large church plants *and* get behind small Christian communities. The two complement each other.

Once a church plant is established, members can start new Christian communities as part of their discipleship. Volunteers from these communities and from the original plant can then start the next "church plant."

In turn, this second plant can spawn small Christian communities, which can help resource the next larger plant.

And so the process continues.

- *Phase 1.* Start a large church plant.
- *Phase 2.* Teach 21st century discipleship. Encourage members to form new Christian communities, and link them to the original plant as congregations of the plant.
- *Phase 3.* Start a second large plant with volunteers from the original plant and its smaller offshoots.
- *Phase 4.* Teach the new plant 21st century discipleship . . . and keep cycling through the process.

In this way, large and small can reinforce and support each other.

Don't settle for one church plant followed a few years later by another. Be more ambitious! Encourage scores of new Christian communities—mini congregations. Celebrate them as carnivals of love in ordinary existence.

Whether you start these new communities as fruits of a church plant, or as branches from your local church, or as trees—new local churches—in their own right, cheer as the Spirit of God transforms the face of society.